THE TRUTH
GOD OR EVOLUTION?

MARSHALL AND SANDRA HALL

BAKER BOOK HOUSE
Grand Rapids, Michigan

Copyright 1974 by
Marshall and Sandra Hall
All rights reserved

Reprinted 1975 by
Baker Book House,
Grand Rapids, Michigan

Formerly published by
The Craig Press,
Nutley, New Jersey

Library of Congress Catalog Card No.: 72-96942
ISBN: 0-8010-4139-2

Contents

About the Authors 5

Foreword 7

Part One
Seven Reasons Why People Believe in
Evolution 9

Part Two
Scientific Evidence That Disproves the
    Theory of Evolution 16
    Spontaneous Generation 16
    Mutations 22
    Natural Selection 32
    Kinds 41
    Fossils 53
    Time 69

Part Three
The Logic of Special Design and Creation 87
    What Is Logical? 87
    Newton's Model 92
    Monkeys, Apes, and the Like........... 94
    Monkeys, etc. 99
    Superlemur 106
    Thumbs 108
    A Strange Tail 109
    The Cow 110
    The Eye 112
    Sam: The Quasi Amphibian—A Farce 114

The Miraculous and the Cambium Layer 119
Form and Structure Similarities 122
Earth—Viewed from the North Star 128
Pollination—A Call to Poets 137
Thirty-six Bristles 138
Three Minus One Equals Two, Minus One
    Equals One 143

Part Four
What Is Next? 145
    Science 145
    Education 155
    Freud's Impact on Modern Behavior 162
    Communism 174
    Philosophy 192
    Final Comment 203

Notes 205

Appendix
    Edward Blyth 217
    Slime Hoax 218
    The Bristlecone Correction 221
    Miscellaneous Evolutionary Humor 222

Bibliography 224

About the Authors

Marshall R. Hall, Jr. (B.S. Cum Laude, M.A.) is a resident Ph.D. student at the Center for Advanced International Studies at the University of Miami, Coral Gables, Florida. He is also the recipient of Fellowships to the University of Denver, the State University of New York at Stony Brook, and Baldwin-Wallace College in Ohio. Upon discovering one unbridgeable gap after another in evolutionary theory, Hall—a previously convinced evolutionist, atheist, and leftist-humanist—turned with his wife to do research on one of the most important truths of all: the truth about the origin of life.

Sandra Sherwood Hall, attended school in China, Portuguese Macao, the Philippines, and Mexico. She also attended Hockaday School in Dallas, Texas, and graduated from Southern Methodist University. She has an M.A. from Middlebury College in Vermont. She has taught at Dade Junior College in Miami, Florida. "This experience," she says of working with her husband on the book, "has led me to a discovery I never thought possible: proof of the existence of a Creator. This is difficult to grasp at first, but I believe that if the book is read slowly—perhaps even aloud—it has the power to convince people that evolution is indeed *not* the way we got here."

Foreword

This book has three goals. One is to destroy the theory of evolution with scientific evidence and logical reasoning. The second is to point out that there are only two theories which attempt to explain the origin of all life—evolution and creation—and that the discrediting of one of these (evolution) logically proves the other (special creation). The third goal is to reveal the wide influence of evolutionary theory in our times, and then to show the world-shaking changes that can be expected once the theory of evolution is thoroughly discredited.

The careful reader may judge whether these goals have been achieved.

Marshall Hall
Sandra Hall

Part One

SEVEN REASONS WHY PEOPLE BELIEVE IN EVOLUTION

Though there is no way of knowing how many people believe in the theory of evolution, there is no question that the figure would be in the tens of millions. Moreover, there are other tens of millions who have a "feeling" that the theory is untrue, but cannot prove it. They probably would be a little embarrassed to admit their "feeling" in the face of such overwhelming "scientific evidence" which they have either heard about or read somewhere.

In short, the theory's impact on the modern world is extensive and virtually unchallenged. Most of us can verify the truth of this statement from our own experience. We know, for example, that large circulation magazines have run prominent articles—complete with charts and drawings—of the course of man's evolution from a microscopic cell in the ocean through his amphibious and mammalian and apelike stages down to his present form of *Homo sapiens*. We know that the schools and universities accept the theory and perpetuate it through books, articles, and lectures. Historically we are aware that a good part of the world's business community welcomed a social-Darwinism that justified a "survival of the fittest." Even many churches accept and promote the theory in some diluted form. Most any self-respecting member of the "intellectual" community will cough on the back of his hand and roll his eyes upward at the thought of one of his journals or colleagues questioning evolution!

Evolution, consequently, is an article of faith in the modern world.

How did it achieve this stature? There are seven good reasons.

First Reason

In the first place, evolution is what is taught in the schools. At least two, and in some cases three and four generations, have used textbooks that presented it as proven fact. The teachers, who for the most part learned it as truth, pass it on as truth. Students are as thoroughly and as surely indoctrinated with the concept of evolution as students have ever been indoctrinated with any unproven belief.

Second Reason

A second powerful persuader, and perhaps the most significant, has been the stamp of approval given to evolution by important spokesmen from not only scientific fields, but from the social sciences, arts, and the humanities as well. Indeed, one can hardly name an important person in any field who has challenged the vulnerable theory in the last fifty years or so. When an exception is given, it is frequently the Scopes Trial of 1925 where William Jennings Bryan won the legal battle but lost the publicity war. How, then, are people with little or no special knowledge of the various sciences and related subjects to challenge the authorities? It is natural to accept what "experts" say, and most people do.

An important factor in perpetuating this reason for belief in the theory of evolution is what might be called *professional respect.* In practice this comes down to an unwritten code that keeps members of the same profession from attacking each other's ideas even if an attack is justified. The cause of this habit is at least threefold: 1) A doesn't attack B or C because he doesn't want to be attacked when he writes something. 2) The profession looks stronger and more certain of itself if internal warfare is kept to a minimum. The profession's prestige is thereby enhanced. 3) It is assumed that in their narrow areas the specialists are experts and are unchallengeable. This attitude is especially prevalent in educational circles.

While this sort of behavior is somewhat natural and relatively harmless in some endeavors, it is inexcusable among the professionals who are supposed to be the fountain of wisdom and goodness from which a thirsty, busy populace can refresh itself with complete confidence that nothing important to their lives is being misrepresented.

Third Reason

A third strong magnet which pulls people away from belief in a Creator and into a willing acceptance of the theory of evolution is the often cruel and immoderate behavior of many organized religions down through history. Whether sacrificing virgins to a sun god or burning witches at the stake or just generally taking advantage of some situations in which they have been, religions—advocates of God and special creation—have too often set a very poor example for sensitive, thinking people to follow.

Fourth Reason

An effort to escape responsibility to a Creator (frequently thought of as being harsh and rigid) accounts for many persons embracing evolutionary theory. With evolution, after all, one is just the temporary end of a long line of fish, frogs, and orangoutangs. It just happened that way; you are not responsible. It makes some activities in life easier to justify. Besides, it seems, so many of the well-educated believe the same thing. And, of course, identification with the views of recognized intellectuals can be very comforting to a lot of people.

Fifth Reason

There is a fifth reason for many people's willingness to accept and even welcome the theory of evolution as a guidepost for the conduct of their lives. We refer here to the widespread and unmistakable presence of "bad" things that go on. Why has there been and why is there still so much suffering, so much injustice in the world? If there is a God, why doesn't He correct the injustices and stop the suffering? These are difficult questions which many religions have attempted to answer with something less than full success.

Yet, while religions often have failed to answer this question satisfactorily, the theory of evolution suggests an answer that seems very reasonable. Even though man and the world about him are just purposeless accidents and everything is basically absurd, the evolutionists say, at least you can understand the "bad" things that go on without falling back on difficult-to-believe concepts. This is a great attraction that evolutionary explanations have over those of many institutionalized religions.

Sixth Reason

A sixth reason is distantly related to number five, but is distinct enough and important enough to warrant separate attention. It has to do with altruism, a regard for and devotion to the interests of others. In its ideal form, those who want to help others shun egoism and selfishness, and frequently work very hard to try to make life as comfortable and meaningful as possible for everyone. Convinced by "science" that man is just another animal—a meaningless cosmic accident—they attempt to maximize rational and humanistic behavior while striving for utopian goals through political and economic reforms. Utopia (an earthly heaven)—or as close to it as man can get—becomes the reason for living. It becomes the humanists' outlet for their passion for truth, justice, freedom. Humanism, atheism, and some form of socialism become their holy trinity. These spread rapidly and break up into sects with their saints and prophets, rules and regulations, sacred writings and rituals, greater and lesser holy places. All who follow this path *with open eyes* can see altruism turning to ashes. But in a world made meaningless by evolution, a person who wants to do good may well see this as the only reasonable course open that gives some purpose to life.

Seventh Reason

There is a seventh reason why many people believe in the theory of evolution. Like the other six, it has nothing whatsoever to do with the actual truth or falsity of the theory itself, but is, rather, merely another explanation of why the theory is attractive to many.

Basically, this reason rests on the idea that while there is no *proof* of God, the evolution theory does offer proof for its position. The purpose of this book is to make it *impossible for anyone to say that there is scientific proof of evolution.* When that stage is reached in a person's mind, he or she may then decide if all that we are and all that is gives *proof* of God or not.

Any one of these seven reasons is, by itself, strong enough to attract people to a way of life based on the theory of evolution. Taken together they are often irresistible. However, a great many people actively opposed this theory and resisted the siren's call in all of these appeals. Since there is *no evidence whatsoever* that proves the evolutionist's notions that life is a cosmic accident, and since there is abundant evidence to show that it is not an accident, those people may yet have their look of skepticism rewarded.

Summary—Seven Reasons Why People Believe in Evolution

1. It has been taught exclusively for two generations or more in most schools.
2. Most authorities from the sciences and other fields support the theory in books, magazines, lectures, etc.
3. Organized religions' record of intolerance and superstition drives many people to accept evolutionary answers.
4. An accidental, absurd world provides a convenient escape from certain moral responsibilities. The question becomes "If, in the final analysis, nothing really matters, then why not do whatever seems attractive?"
5. The presence of evil in the world seems to rule out an all-powerful Creator.
6. Secular religions (Humanism, Communism, Utopian-Socialism, etc.) have become institutionalized. They have faithful followers, rites, saints, martyrs, sacred writings, holy places, and interests to protect. The evolutionary commandment—life is accidental and basically purposeless—is the basis of their need to exist.
7. There seems to be no proof of God. Evolutionists *seem* to offer proof for their position.

Though we have listed seven reasons why people believe in evolution, it is clear that reason number two—weight of scientific authority—is of primary importance. If the credibility of these authorities and their "evidence" can be undermined, the reasons for believing in evolution will fall of their own weight, having had their main support removed.

So, let us begin undermining.

Part Two

SCIENTIFIC EVIDENCE THAT DISPROVES THE THEORY OF EVOLUTION

What follows in this chapter are examples of *scientific contradiction, retreat, confusion, and guesswork* that form "supports" of the theory of evolution. The reader can decide if this is a theory that deserves to be called scientific.

The sub-headings are: 1) spontaneous generation, 2) mutations, 3) natural selection, 4) kinds, 5) fossils, and 6) time.

These subheadings are only meant to be rough boundaries. Quite often one topic spills over into another. With that qualification let us look first at *spontaneous generation.*

Spontaneous Generation

Spontaneous generation is "the generation of living from nonliving matter ... [it is taken] from a belief, now abandoned, that organisms found in putrid organic matter arose spontaneously from it" (Webster's).

"A belief, now abandoned...." (What a familiar phrase that will get to be!) Francesco Redi (c. 1688) disproved the idea of spontaneous generation through experimentation. Lazzaro Spallanzani (c. 1780) did the same thing. Louis Pasteur (c. 1860) settled the question once and for all in a famous debate with Pusche. Modern scientists are mostly in agreement that spontaneous generation is "a belief now abandoned...."

"So what?" someone could ask. "Everybody knows that scientists have shown that maggots and flies won't develop out of dead matter if the microorganisms are killed and the dead matter is sealed. Nobody believes that horse hairs turn into snakes anymore or that flies come into existence from decaying matter.* All those beliefs have been abandoned...."

And so they have. The only problem with abandoning the concept is that *there could have been no evolution without spontaneous generation!* Two *billion* years ago or so, according to evolutionists, there was no life on land or in the sea. There was only nonliving matter. Then, when conditions became right, say the evolutionists, this nonliving matter produced living matter which has since evolved into all known living things, including man. The following quotation captures the current acceptable "scientific" view as well as any:

> The spontaneous generation origin of living things at the present time is believed to be extremely improbable. Yet that this same event occurred in the past is quite probable. The difference lies in the conditions existing on earth, then as opposed to now.... The postulated origin of living matter *assumes* the occurrence of a chemical evolution[1] (our emphasis).

All the laboratory efforts to create living matter

---

*"People once believed that new generations of living things arose from nonliving matter. For example, snakes were believed to arise from horsehairs and flies from decaying meat. This false idea about the production of living things was called *spontaneous generation*," (Review Text in *Life Science*, by Milton S. Lesser, Amsco School Publications, Inc., p. 255).

from nonliving matter have failed. All efforts to bring about spontaneous generation have failed. But clearly, if scientists are to be able to say that spontaneous generation is indeed what happened, then the laws that govern life must be assumed to have been different whenever they *had* to be to make the theory possible. This won't do, obviously, because the whole of evolutionary theory rests on the assumption that conditions on the earth have remained uniform throughout evolution.

Evolutionists are saying that all the indescribably complex life that makes up our own being and is all around us in well over a million forms—that all this started from spontaneous generation out of nonliving matter. The process to which they attribute all life cannot be duplicated in the laboratory, and cannot be observed going on now. Everything the evolutionists say violates not only what is known, it violates something more convincing to an individual, that is, his own human intuition, his own common sense, his own natural logic, or whatever you want to call it. The more it is violated by something trying to be what it isn't and can't be, the more set against that something it becomes. When this common sense unites with factual evidence, a thought must be born. And the facts you will see in virtually every quotation in this book prove that evolutionists not only must assume everything (that's okay)—but they must assume everything happened in ways that go against *all* the scientific evidence and laws of probability. *All* of it! Keep this in mind as your common sense begins to work on these different areas.

Keep in mind, for example, that a "simple" cell of the type that spontaneously generated itself (in spite of the fact that it can't) is more complicated than any man-made thing on earth! Even the complexity of New York City (bricks, wires, glass, machines) is less complicated than the structure of this simplest microscopic life that evolutionists tell us came together accidentally out of nonliving matter.*

But neither all this complexity, nor the fact that it can't be done now, bothers the faithful. And the faithful gathered at Chicago in 1959 to celebrate the one hundredth anniversary of the prophet Darwin's publication of holy writ. One amongst them spake:

> ... the origin of life presupposes first of all, the natural accumulation of suitable raw materials. ... Further presupposed is a gradual evolution of increasingly complex systems from the raw materials until a self-contained unit appears which we would be willing to recognize as a living thing.[2]

And all who were gathered there nodded approval, so that the same wise one spoke again:

> The assumption that life originated from nonliving matter must be made by the modern scientist if he believes that the question "What is life?" belongs in the natural sciences at all. ...[3]

"The assumption ... must be made ... " or no evolution, right? Very well. But let us keep in the front of our minds that this is an assumption that goes against all known laws; an assumption that is based on a mathematical probability that is next to zero; an assumption that asserts itself as reasonable only because evolutionary scientists will not deal with another reality as mind-boggling as life. They ignore as irrelevant the fact that the existence of earth, light, water, atmosphere, universe, was all there *before* their impossible myth was

---

*Every minute in the human body, 3 billion cells die and 3 billion are born.

supposed to have begun. They call irrelevant all that without which there could be no life. We find that a peculiar attitude. Notice this chemist's answer to the search for life, and the way he avoids obvious and crucial questions:

> The compounds which abounded in the primeval seas on our cooling planet and were therefore available to serve as the building units for the edifice of life were thus selected for their roles by a process of atomic evolution.[4]

"Selected for their roles by atomic evolution"—very clever of atomic evolution, wouldn't you say? Unbelievably clever, be assured, when a few sentences earlier—after discussion of various compounds—you could have read:

> But most of these compounds are too unstable to exist for more than fractions of a second.[5]

More stable compounds are needed obviously, and "the governing principle of this (atomic) evolution might be said to be: 'The survival of the stablest.' "[6] Competitive atoms! Competing for what? With what? Darwin's "survival of the fittest"—an embarrassment to modern biologists—is now apparently driven to its true home, chemistry. But where is the competition when a molecular compound like Adenine (which "withstands with impunity cooking with concentrated acid") is put up against compounds that are "too unstable to exist for more than fractions of a second"?!

But, no matter, you grow accustomed to this sort of double-talk when you read about evolution. So, we find, the next step in the spontaneous generation of life moves right along when the stable compounds get into big complex bunches in the water (spontaneously generated water??). The process grows more involved—molecule elimination, detachment of hydrogen and hydroxyl units, molecular fusion—until we get what is called a dimer, a double unit of two fused molecules. From there on out it is a cinch:

> ...such a dimer can also undergo a similar accretive fusion and that is how the nucleic acids and the proteins, substances of infinite complexity and wondrous potency, are built by that fabulous architect: a living cell.[7]

Notice the *"can* also undergo," not *"does* also undergo." And what is the "fabulous architect" of all this "infinite complexity and wondrous potency?" A living cell. Right? And what is a living cell? "Nucleic acids and proteins, substances of infinite complexity and wondrous potency," right? So we have a marvelous example of circular reasoning: A = B and, furthermore, B = A. The logic of evolutionary scientists is beautiful. Every bit of it. But we did like his term "fabulous architect." We are going to capitalize it and steal it, and use it in other places. Fabulous Architect! Now there's a Builder!

But, of course, it's unscientific to speak of something such as a Fabulous Architect (God), because—now get this—because such a complex entity couldn't have come out of nothing.... Evolutionary scientists are willing to bend natural laws, manufacture abstruse and impossible theories, go to any length to deny God and to see that everybody else does, so we can have an absurd world where *they* can function because they are absurd people. They say that spontaneous generation had to happen. It doesn't. It hasn't. It won't. It can't. But it did. They say.

Yet—if evolutionary scientists can accept *their* concept of the impossible—why can't they accept *creation ex nihilo by a Creator* who put all this "infinite complexity and wondrous potency" here and made it work as it does?!

We do not know why one is possible and the other isn't, unless certain scientists make it that way!

But let us press on.

The simplest living cell is unbelievably intricate and structured, scientists agree. It came out of nonliving matter, evolutionists agree. This is ontogenesis, i.e., self-generation. It is also abiogenesis, which also means self-generated. And they all are the same as spontaneous generation.

Scientists demand that spontaneous generation be possible so that their theory of the origin of life can be validated. The same scientists refuse to allow other intelligent people to demand that spontaneous generation be possible so that their theory of the origin of God can be validated. Scientists are funny people; at least the evolutionary ones. We say this because:

> To today's biologist, with his extended knowledge of the intricate physicochemical complexity of the living cell, the sudden, spontaneous appearance of even a simple living organism is inconceivable. . . .[8]

Summary—Spontaneous Generation

1. There had to be spontaneous generation for evolution to have begun.
2. The concept of spontaneous generation is "a belief, now abandoned" by scientists for at least a hundred years.

Mutations

There are three necessary parts to the theory of evolution. Take any one of them away and the theory has the same scientific credibility as the tooth fairy. You have just examined one of those vital parts—spontaneous generation; and now we can proceed to a second necessary part of the theory, viz., mutations.

In 1895, a Dutch botanist named Hugo De Vries made an interesting discovery. He had been studying flowers called evening primroses, when he noticed that one of them was different from the others, although it evidently came from the same seeds. He planted seeds from the odd specimen and it produced plants like itself. De Vries concluded that the flower was a new species that had arisen as a result of some sudden change in the germ plasm. He called it a *mutation*.

Gradually, since De Vries's discovery, the main vehicle for carrying the theory of evolution has come to be *mutations* or *sports* as they used to be called. A mutation is change, and change is what evolution is all about.

First, let us make no mistake that mutations are currently the main reason given for what causes evolution to happen:

> What then do present day evolutionists appeal to for the mechanism of evolution? The answer is mutations which occur with varying frequency in plants and animals.[9]

Sir Julian Huxley, one of a dozen or so of the principal spokesmen for evolutionary theory in the twentieth century, described the necessity of the De Vries's discovery to the modern theory:

> Mutation ... provides the raw material of evolution; it is a random affair and takes place in all directions.[10]

A few pages earlier he had expressed the necessity even more strongly. There, he said:

> ... mutation is the ultimate source of all ... heritable variation.[11]

Examples could be multiplied, but the message would still be the same, and that message is that mutations are considered necessary for evolution to have occurred. Nevertheless, it is possible to show beyond any doubt that this key point in the theory of evolution has no claim whatever to be called scientific. Let us examine several kinds of evidence.

First of all, there are two facts that cast grave doubts on the ability of mutations to bring about changes any more obvious than what De Vries saw. One of the facts is that mutations are *very rare*. Only about "one in a hundred thousand,"[12] Huxley guesses, is a mutant. The other fact about mutations is that when one finally does occur, it is almost certain to be harmful or deadly, a proposition that leads to extinction rather than evolution. Huxley admits:

> ... the great majority of mutant genes are harmful in their effects on the organism.[13]

Permit us to carry this point further than Sir Julian is understandably willing to carry it. In John J. Fried's book, *The Mystery of Heredity,* this observation about mutations gives a better picture of their true character:

> We have to face one particular fact, one so peculiar that in the opinion of some people it makes nonsense of the whole theory of evolution: Although the biological theory calls for incorporation of beneficial variants in the living populations, a vast majority of the mutants observed in any organism are detrimental to its welfare. Some are lethal, causing incurable diseases or fatal deaths [*sic*]; others are sub-lethal, killing off or incapacitating

> most of the carriers but allowing some to escape; still others are sub-vital, damaging health, resistance or vigor in a variety of ways.[14]

Are you beginning to see how convincing this vital aspect of evolutionary theory is?! But there is more. Much more! Professor Dobzhansky, another one of the top dozen evolutionists of this century, notes:

> Mutations have been studied for more than a half-century; much has been learned, and yet a geneticist is constrained to admit that his knowledge is decidedly inadequate.[15]

The above comment appeared in a book called *A Book That Shook the World*, an appropriate reference—as will become evident further on—to Darwin's *Origin of Species*.

Genetics came along more than a generation after Darwin published his book in 1859, so it is useful to see what the father of evolutionary theory himself thought about the all-important question of mutations. He was aware of these occasional changes, and he called them *sports* or *variations* and regarded them "simply as curiosities." In fact, he

> ... did not consider them important because they nearly always represented obviously disadvantageous modifications from the point of view of the struggle for existence; consequently they would most likely be rapidly eliminated in the wild state by the operation of natural selection.[16]

"This," comments Professor Caullery, "is almost exactly what happens."[17] An honorary professor at the Sorbonne when he made that observation, Professor Caullery gave this view in the same book as to the connection of mutations with evolution:

> ... it must be remembered that the vast majority of these mutations, whether natural or artificially produced, are recessive, and would therefore remain dormant under natural conditions, and almost all are degenerate in kind and would therefore be rapidly eliminated by natural selection.[18]

After calling attention to the failure to produce a new species of the fly *Drosophila melanogaster* even with heroic attempts at artificially produced mutation (see Part Three—Thirty-six Bristles, pp. 138-143), the professor concludes that:

> It does not seem, therefore, that the central problem of evolution can be solved by mutations.[19]

Professor Ernst Mayr, in his exhaustive study *Animal Species and Evolution,* seems to go back and forth on the question of the importance of mutations. On an early page, he says:

> We now believe that mutations do not guide evolution. . . .[20]

Yet, 170 pages further along, he changes key in the middle of the tune:

> Various exaggerated claims of the immediate evolutionary importance of mutations are thus not valid. [Almost the same as before; right? Now notice:] Yet it must not be forgotten that mutation is the ultimate source of all genetic variation found in natural populations and the only raw material available for natural selection to work on.[21]

The sort of confusion that is obvious in this remark and others on the last few pages is really quite understandable. The problem, you see, is this: Darwin's main ideas had all been torpedoed, and the idea of mutations became one of the three essential props of the theory (along with spontaneous generation and natural selection). Now, faced with the fact that they have *no convincing evidence whatsoever* to support their claims about mutations, evolutionary scientists are understandably a little less than coherent when they deal with the subject. Struggling admirably with his topic, Professor Simpson explores the outer limits of the subject of mutations. In part of a paragraph (included in full below), he writes about multiple, simultaneous mutations and reports that the mathematical likelihood of getting good evolutionary results would occur only once in about 274 billion years. "Obviously," he concludes, "such a process has played no part whatever in evolution."

> The chances of multiple, simultaneous mutation seem to be even smaller, indeed negligible. Postulation of a mutation rate of .00001 and of each mutation's doubling the chances of another in the same nucleus would correspond with the most favorable circumstances warranted by laboratory evidence. Under these postulates, the probability of five mutations in the same nucleus would be approximately 10^{-22}. With an average effective breeding population of 100 million individuals and an average length of generation of one day, again extremely favorable postulates, such an event would be expected only once in about 274 billion years, or about a hundred times the probable age of the earth. Obviously, unless there is an unknown factor tremendously increasing the chance of simultaneous mutations, such a process has played no part whatever in evolution.[22]

What we would like to call to your attention is that there are books written by evolutionists full of abstruse "explanations" such as this one that show how evolution did not happen, and could not have happened.

You may wonder, as we do (as anyone would!), why evolutionists plunge into these statistical blind alleys if they have any proof *for* their theory!

In any case, a fair summation of the basic question of the role and importance of mutations comes down to this: 1) Mutations do not and cannot solve the main problem of evolution, that is, they do not and cannot supply the critical answer as to how the necessary changes occur; but, 2) mutations *must* solve this problem because they are the only source of such change.

Evolutionary logic is wonderful, isn't it?!

But, all is not lost. "Gene recombination" joins in the battle alongside the mortally wounded new standard-bearer, mutation. Professor Mayr is sure that this is where the truth lies now. He writes:

> Recombination . . . is by far the most important source of genetic variation . . . [and] genotype variation is of critical importance in evolution.[23]

This, he warns those who are still plugging for mutations and natural selection,

> . . . may be quite startling to those who are unaware of the modern developments and who are still fighting the fight of the last generation.[24]

Dobzhansky backs him up:

> In organisms which reproduce sexually [this rules out all the earliest so-called evolutionary forms of life] the process of gene recombination is even more important than that of mutations as a cause of the genetic diversity of individuals, and conse-

quently as a source of the raw materials of evolution.... Most of the mutant genes which are components of the genetic loads may be harmful, but occasionally a constellation of genes may be formed which will be useful.[25]

"Most ... may be harmful ..."—that means virtually all *are* harmful. "Occasionally" and "may be" are the kind of strong scientific expressions that are standard in the evolutionists' vocabulary. Nevertheless, though Mayr and Dobzhansky now place their hopes for the mechanics of evolution on gene recombination, bacteriologist, Dr. Burns takes quite another view of the same process. "Recombination," he says,

... merely redistributes existing genetic material among different individuals; it *makes no change in it*[26] (our emphasis).

Burns goes further:

The mechanism whereby chromosomal segment and its genes become incorporated into the recipient's chromosome is *not understood* but two major theories have been proposed: a) copy-choice, and b) break and exchange.... Neither theory is fully acceptable ...[27] (our emphasis).

Professor Mayr seems to agree about the two theories and the uncertainties surrounding their operation. The concept of *linkage* in the crossing over of chromosomes is important, even critical, to recombination, he judges, but as it turns out:

... on the whole linkage is a rather inefficient mechanism for the preservation of genetic variation.[28]

Thus, it appears, the rickety vehicle that is supposed to carry the theory of evolution has broken down again. It is obvious that it is beyond effective repair and will soon have to be junked.

Professor Mayr, certainly among the most learned of the evolutionists, is—like all his evolutionist colleagues—constantly driven to qualify even the tiniest of points in a theory long ago stretched beyond any inkling of scientific credibility. Darwin, as L. M. Davies has shown, used over eight hundred phrases in the subjunctive mood ("Let us assume," "If one accepts," etc.) in *The Origin of Species*, a 525-page book. In a random check of 10 pages from Mayr's *Animal Species and Evolution* we found seventeen instances of such subjunctive language indicating various degrees of doubt, uncertainty, incomplete evidence, and obvious speculation. With this ratio sustained for the 662 pages of the book, he would have some 1125 scientifically flabby thoughts, thus considerably outdoing Darwin in this regard. Simpson and all the other evolutionist authors rank very high in this respect too, whether the subject be mutations or any other aspect of the theory.

It is a great pity and a great loss that so much brainpower should be wasted trying to reconcile the irreconcilable!

But rather than announce to the world that the weaknesses of the theory have grown with the years to the point that no one can even defend the vital mutations concept, evolutionists grind out ever more rarefied theories, only to resign them to the scrap heap a few years later—unbeknownst to the general public.

If we are not mistaken, though, there is restless stirring among the people. It is evident by the increasing number of scholarly, well-trained scientists* who have authored antievolutionary books and/or who are creationists in key teaching or industrial positions, by the demands of biology teachers in California that the creation theory be given equal time, and by other signs. Many people sense that a huge and not very funny hoax passing under the name of science has been perpetrated upon them. They are 100 percent right in this feeling, as we believe the following material will attest. False

---

*Such men include *Harold Armstrong,* Physical Science, Queens University, Kingston, Ontario; *Thomas G. Barnes,* Physics, University of Texas (El Paso); *Edward F. Blick,* Aerospace, Mechanical, and Nuclear Engineering, University of Oklahoma; *David R. Boylan,* Dean, College of Engineering, Iowa State University; *Larry G. Butler,* Biochemistry, Purdue University; *Donald E. Chittick,* Physical Chemistry, George Fox College, Newberg, Oregon; *Kenneth B. Cumming,* Research Biologist, Fish Control Laboratory, La Crosse, Wisconsin; *H. Douglas Dean,* Biological Science, Pepperdine College, Los Angeles; *Duane T. Gish,* Associate Director of the Institute for Creation Research and formerly in biochemical and biomedical research at the Upjohn Company; *Donald D. Hamann,* Food Technology, North Carolina State University; *Charles W. Harrison, Jr.,* Director, General Electro-Magnetics, Albuquerque; *Harold R. Henry,* Chairman of Civil and Mining Engineering Department, University of Alabama; *Joseph L. Henson,* Chairman of Science Division, Bob Jones University; *George F. Howe,* Biological Science, Los Angeles Baptist College; *R. Clyde McCone,* Anthropology, California State University, Long Beach; *John R. Meyer,* Biological Science, University of Louisville (Kentucky); *John N. Moore,* Natural Science, Michigan State University; *Henry M. Morris,* Director of the Institute for Creation Research and formerly Chairman of the Civil Engineering Department at the Virginia Polytechnic Institute and State University; *Wilbert H. Rusch, Sr.,* Biological Science, Concordia Lutheran College, Ann Arbor, Michigan; and *Harold S. Slusher,* Chairman of the Department of Planetary Science at Christian Heritage College and formerly at the University of Texas (El Paso) as Director of Kidd Memorial Seismic Observatory and in charge of the University's curricula in Geophysics and Astrophysics.

theories—especially those with deep impact on the lives of the unsuspecting—cannot be laid to rest too soon.

Summary—Mutations

1. Present-day evolutionists credit mutations with being the raw material of evolution.
2. Almost all mutations are harmful or deadly. Yet, for evolution to happen, they must be favorable and heritable.
3. Confusion reigns among the evolutionists about the significance of mutations. Some say mutations are the main thing; others say no.
4. Some evolutionists have retreated from mutations to "gene recombinations" as the answer for evolution. Others declare that this process merely redistributes genetic material; it does not change it. And *change* is demanded for evolution theory.
5. Evolutionary scientists use unscientific language. It is mainly postulations, speculations, and extrapolations.
6. Evolutionary theory has come to rely on mutations for the answers it *must* have. Mutations theory is *scientifically* incapable of accounting for evolution of the world's plant and animal species.
7. The death of the mutations theory means the death of evolutionary theory.

Natural Selection

The concept of "natural selection" is the same thing as "survival of the fittest," but the former term is more in vogue with evolutionary scientists. This is too bad in a way, it seems to us. "Survival of the fittest" is the kind of expression nonscientists can understand, and if everyone is to be an evolutionist it would seem that this concept should be as easily understood as it is possible to make it. For, after all, "survival of the fittest" along with spontaneous generation and mutations is one of the three *essential* ingredients of evolutionary thought.*

Darwin himself titled his chapter on this subject: "Natural Selection; or The Survival of the Fittest." The second part of the title was borrowed from Herbert Spencer, who had used the expression in 1852 along with another expression that Darwin liked and borrowed, viz., the "Struggle for Existence."

In fact, it appears that Darwin "borrowed" just about everything he wrote in *The Origin of Species.* Simpson, a leader among modern evolutionists, says as much:

> ... there is practically nothing in Darwin's theories that had not been expressed by others long before him.[29]

Certainly Darwin appears to have been aware of the essays that Edward Blyth had written on the subject of natural selection. These were published in 1835, 1836, and 1837—over twenty years before Darwin published the *Origin.* Darwin knew Blyth, corresponded with him, and was quite interested in his studies of animal variation. Yet Darwin never made reference to Blyth's essays on natural selection. The fact that he did not do so

> ... may have been because Blyth used the theory of natural selection not to explain how species can arise from pre-existing species (as Darwin does), but rather to explain how species remain constant.

---

*Natural selection, as defined by Webster, is: "The natural process tending to cause the 'survival of the fittest' (that is, the survival of those forms of animals and plants best adjusted to the conditions under which they live), and extinction of poorly adapted forms." Darwin considered natural selection as the most important factor in organic evolution.

The action of selection, he thought, would serve to eliminate not only monsters, but all deviants from the norm, all the abnormal types that arise in every population; and so it would make each species hold true to type, and stay fit to continue its existence within the given environment.[30] (See Appendix "Edward Blyth," page 217, for a somewhat fuller account.)

Darwin, of course, turned Blyth's idea on natural selection around no less than 180 degrees. Instead of natural selection serving to keep the species constant, Darwin made it into *the* way that change or evolution took place.

Embarrassingly, Darwin found himself at opposite poles on the question of natural selection and struggle for existence with none other than the co-founder of modern evolution theory, Alfred Russel Wallace.* Wallace parted ways with his more famous colleague over the issue of natural selection. Observing that supposedly backward natives had languages more complicated than those of modern Europe, and that "their mental powers were far in excess of what they really needed to carry on the simple food-gathering techniques by which they survive," Wallace asked:

---

*Alfred R. Wallace (1823-1913) "flashed on the idea of the survival of the fittest." He sent a draft to Darwin and in July 1858, Darwin presented the joint paper. "Wallace differed from Darwin on the problem of human evolution. He considered that natural selection was *not* sufficient to explain certain features of man's structure such as the loss of hair and the specialized character of the hands and feet. He was also of the opinion that man's mental faculties could not be regarded as a product of natural selection.... The operation of natural selection would ... have been such as to oppose the action of sexual selection and hence it followed that 'this extremely rigid action of natural selection must render any attempt to select mere orna-

> How, then, was an organ developed so far beyond the needs of its possessor? Natural selection could only have endowed the savage with a brain a little superior to that of an ape, whereas he actually possesses one but little inferior to that of the average member of our learned societies.[31]

Wallace (the man who launched the evolution theory simultaneously with Darwin, remember!) went farther. Anthropologist and naturalist Loren Eiseley explains:

> Finally, Wallace challenged the whole Darwinian position on man by insisting that artistic, mathematical, and musical abilities could not be explained on the basis of natural selection and the struggle for existence. Something else, he contended, some unknown spiritual element must have been at work in the elaboration of the human brain. Why else would men of simple cultures possess the basic intellectual powers which the Darwinists maintained could be elaborated only by competitive struggle?[32]

Darwin was shaken by the heresy of his colleague, *but he never took up the challenge.* If he had, maybe the

---

ment (as in the case of color differences found in the two sexes of the same animal species) utterly nugatory, unless the most ornamented always coincide with the fittest in every respect; while if they do so coincide, then any selection of ornament is altogether superfluous.'" Though he rejected revealed religion, he wrote a book entitled *Miracles and Modern Spiritualism* (1881) which "gave an account of the experimental evidence which led him to spiritualistic beliefs.... His sympathetic personality is reflected in the fact that he never attempted to conceal the magnitude of Darwin's contribution to the theory developed *independently* by *both* men" (*Chamber's Encyclopedia,* vol. 14, New York: Maxwell Scientific International, Inc., 1967, p. 392).

question of natural selection (survival of the fittest) would have been threshed out long before now. And this would have been useful because—although the average citizen doesn't know anything about it—the other main supports that Darwin used to build his theory have all been knocked down. As author Joseph Wood Krutch summed up in the Darwinian centennial year, 1959:

> ... the fact remains that Darwin was able to convince both himself and others that his theory was tenable only by calling to its support *three assumptions now completely exploded:* 1) that acquired characteristics are inherited—a heresy even the most unorthodox would hesitate to advance today; 2) that "sexual selection," now almost as thoroughly discredited, played an important role; and 3) that the variations later selected for survival were supplied by an innate tendency of all organisms to slight variations—instead, as modern biologists believe, by the relatively large "mutations" of whose existence Darwin took no account.[33]

Let us examine further, then, the remaining crutch of the evolutionists, natural selection. How important is it to the theory? Sir Julian Huxley makes his position clear:

> So far as we know ... *natural selection ... is the only effective agency of evolution* [our emphasis]. What this means ... is that all the theories lumped together under the heads of orthogenesis (change without natural selection) and Lamarckism are invalidated. ... They are *out:* They are no longer consistent with the facts. They have now only a historical interest.[34]

So Huxley says "natural selection is *the only* effective agency of evolution." Contrast this with heavyweight evolutionist, Ernst Mayr's statement:

> Natural selection is no longer regarded as an all-or-none process but rather as a purely statistical concept.[35]

Opposite views, correct?! Lest you think Mayr may be alone in giving up on natural selection, take note of this comment by George Gaylord Simpson, whom you've met, but who "in the opinion of many of the world's leading scientists, stands alone as an interpreter of evolutionary theory":[36]

> Search for *the* cause of evolution has been abandoned. It is now clear that evolution has no single or simple cause.[37]

Huxley says natural selection is the only cause; Mayr says No; Simpson says there is no one cause. Sir Gavin De Beer, "eminent British scientist," sides with Huxley:

> ... so only natural selection is left, and it is selection, not mutation, that controls evolution.[38]

But evolutionary biologist Jean Rostand doesn't believe natural selection is up to the task:

> No, decidedly I cannot make myself think that these slips of heredity (mutations) have been able, even with the cooperation of natural selection, even with the advantage of immense periods of time in which evolution works on life, to build the entire world, with its structural prodigality and refinements, its astounding adaptations.[39]

Sir James Gray, well-known evolutionist, says it is either natural selection that causes evolution or it isn't, and "your guess is as good as mine."[40] Simpson, in yet another book, says of natural selection, that

> ... it might be argued that the theory is quite unsubstantiated and has status only as a speculation.[41]

Huxley is driven to a circular argument on the question. Note:

> On the basis of our present knowledge, natural selection is bound to produce genetic adaptations: and genetic adaptations are thus presumptive evidence for the efficacy of natural selection.[42]

Isn't that beautiful?! A = B, so therefore B = A! We were very impressed, as we are sure you are!

But, let Sir Julian explain natural selection himself:

> To sum up, natural selection converts randomness into direction, and blind chance into apparent purpose. It operates with the aid of time to produce improvements in the machinery of living, and in the process generates results of a more than astronomical improbability which could have been achieved in no other way.[43]

The admission of *more than astronomical improbability* followed by the assertion that there could have been *no other way* has a rather unscientific ring to it, you might say, but Huxley explains both by consulting a mathematician (Muller) who was able to estimate the likelihood of all the necessary developments and combinations of favorable mutations, etc., coming to pass by pure chance in nature to produce a *horse*. Sir Julian reported those findings. If you read the estimate carefully, the mathematical possibility of evolution will be seen to be effectively zero:

... the figure 1 with three million noughts after it: and that would take three large volumes of about five hundred pages each, just to print! ... No one would bet on anything so improbable happening; and yet it *has* happened.[44]*

And, let us remind you who find such odds *ridiculous* (even if you are reassured by Mr. Huxley), that this figure was calculated for the evolution of a *horse!* How many more *volumes* of zeros would be required to give us some idea of the *astronomical improbability* required by Mr. Huxley to produce a *human being?* And then you would have just one horse and one human being, and, unless the mathematician wishes to add in the probability for the evolution of all the plants and animals that are necessary to support a horse and a man, you would have a sterile world where neither could have survived any stage of its supposed evolution! What have we now— the figure 1 followed by a thousand volumes of zeros? Then add another thousand volumes for the improbability of the earth having all the necessary properties for life built into it. And add another thousand volumes for the improbability of the sun, and our orbit, and our daily rotation and the moon and the stars. Add other thousands for the evolution of all the thoughts that man can have, all the objective and subjective reality that ebbs and flows in us like part of the pulsebeat of an inscrutable cosmos!

Add them all in and you long ago stopped talking about rational thought, much less scientific evidence. Yet, Simpson, Huxley, Dobzhansky, Mayr, and dozens

---

*Stated as a decimal this figure would be represented by a decimal point (.) followed by typed zeros that would stretch more than the length of *fifty-five football fields,* then the numeral 1!

of others continue to tell us that that's the way *it had* to be! They have retreated from all the points which ever lent any semblence of credibility to the evolutionary theory. Now they busy themselves with esoteric mathematical formulations based on population genetics, random drift, isolation, and other ploys which have a probability of accounting for life on earth of *minus* zero! They clutter our libraries and press on the minds of people everywhere an animated waxen image of a theory that has been dead for over a decade.

Evolution has no claim whatsoever to being a science.

It is time all this nonsense ceased. It is time to bury the corpse. It is time to shift the books to the humorous fiction section of the libraries.

Summary—Natural Selection

1. "Survival of the fittest" is the same thing as natural selection. Darwin considered this idea the most important factor in evolution.
2. Other important scientists in Darwin's time (including A. R. Wallace, the co-founder of evolutionary theory with Darwin) rejected natural selection as an explanation for evolution.
3. All of Darwin's assumptions are "now completely exploded."
4. Evolutionary "scientists" take contradictory stands on the issue of natural selection. What was regarded as "the only effective agency of evolution" is now regarded "as a purely statistical concept."
5. A decimal point, followed by three miles of typed zeros and the figure *one* (1) at the *end* of the zeros, represents the calculated mathematical odds against the evolution of a horse!

6. Evolution has no claim whatsoever to being a science.

Kinds

The concepts of spontaneous generation, natural selection, and mutations make up what is referred to as the "synthetic theory." (It is interesting that synthetic also means artificial, as well as a synthesis!) Together they carry the burden for proving the general theory of evolution. And, as Simpson says:

> This general theory is now supported by an imposing array of paleontologists, geneticists, and other biological specialists. Differences of opinion on relatively minor points naturally persist and many details remain to be filled in, but the essentials of the explanation of the history of life have probably now been achieved.[45]

You have had some exposure to each of the three main supports of the theory and you might rightly wonder who this "imposing array" of evolutionists think they are kidding! Another and much larger "imposing array" of people who know a dead duck when they see one are going to require in the very near future a lot more solid scientific evidence than any evolutionist has ever given or can ever give. The proverbial handwriting is on the wall. The time to settle this issue is at hand.

If antievolutionists are only wise enough to stick to a scientific and logical attack, they will triumph over this greatest of all stumbling blocks to believing in God. Evolution is scientifically impossible, and this is the fact that must be hammered home, especially to the intelligentsia. We urge people to learn some of the basic *scientific arguments* against evolution, and to actively press them on school boards, local radio and TV, and in the newspapers. (To aid in this we are summarizing the details of these arguments at the end of certain topics.)

But now let us turn to kinds.

Kind is an old word with roots in the word *kin*. Scientists do not use *kind* very much, and since "there are more than 1,200,000 species of organisms that have been discovered and named,"[46] it is understandable that several different sorts of classifications are needed.*

Still, it is a useful description—approximately the same as species—and we will use it interchangeably to designate the limits within which man and animals can reproduce young.

The whole story, of course, is that *only like kinds can reproduce*. The law of nature is inflexible on this point. Bears reproduce bears, camels reproduce camels, humans reproduce humans. Some cross-breeding of plants and animals is possible, but not very far out of their classification. Professor Simpson, whose credentials you have already seen, says:

> Cross-breeding ... is almost never satisfactorily possible at the level of the genera, and absolutely never above that level.[47]

Genera, as you saw in the previous footnote, is just one classification removed from intelligent man. (Since recent evidence on Neanderthal Man indicates he was not a subman at all, and since all other supposed ape-men are just fanciful characters from Uncle Charlie's Book of Evolutionary Myths, Simpson's extension of re-

---

*The scientific classification system from the broadest description to the most specific is: kingdom, phylum, class, order, family, genus, species (and sometimes subspecies or variety). For man the classification is: Kingdom, animal; phylum, *Chordata* (subphylum, vertebrata); class, mammalia; order, primates; family, *Hominidae;* genus, *Homo;* species, sapiens.

production capabilities to genera, it should be noted, excludes man.)

Concerning man, we find:

> Every person on earth today, civilized or primitive, is descended from the same human stock and belongs to the same species.[48]

Evolutionist Gavin De Beer notes in his book on Darwin:

> ... one species does not grow from the seed of another species.[49]

No one, as far as we know, disagrees with this law of nature. Yet, for evolution to have occurred, this law had to be bent, broken, twisted, and finally discarded an absolute mathematical minimum of 1,200,000 times in order to account for the 1,200,000 species that have been classified!

How do evolutionists meet this sledgehammer wallop to their theory? Well, in the first place, people aren't supposed to be talking about such things. Scientists—an "imposing array" of them—have succeeded in assuring the "intellectual" world, at least, that they *know* that evolution occurred much as they say. So why bring up the subject anyway? There may *seem* to be separate deadly reasons why evolution couldn't have happened, but they just *seem* that way because you don't have the overall picture; your faith in the evolutionary scientists' religion is impure. If there were no evolutionary answer, that would imply there was a Creator, Someone smarter than an evolutionary scientist! And you know that couldn't be!

So, how do they meet the challenge? They don't, unless you could call this sort of double-talk an answer:

> Species apparently do frequently arise from sub-

species, but few subspecies become species, and it often happens that species are not, strictly, derived from a single subspecies.[50]

Your libraries are bulging with such models of clarity on the subject of evolution. Go read a few. See for yourself! This same author says in another book on page 143: "... proof that evolution did occur ... was hardly needed after 1880." Then, six pages later he says,

> ... Explanations are ... complete ... up to a certain point but ... it still leaves deeper problems unsolved ... it does not explain why mutations arise or why and how they produce their particular effects. These problems have not yet been solved, although progress is being made and there is every reason to think that they are soluble.[51]

Let us next look together at an extremely complicated subject that bears on the question of kinds, i.e., the subject of genetics.

Webster's tells us that *genetics* is "the branch of biology dealing with heredity and variation among related organisms, largely in their evolutionary aspects...." (When genetics is applied to improving plant and animal strains, breeds, etc., the name becomes *eugenics,* which we will get to later.)

The most important discovery geneticists have come up with is DNA (deoxyribonucleic acid). This abbreviation stands for something that holds the secrets of life itself. Some appreciation of DNA's nature and role in the life process is needed before going further. From a book appropriately titled *The Mystery of Heredity* we learn—if we *read slowly* and reread sometimes, aloud even!—about a force at the root of life:

> In the simplest of one-cell organisms it [DNA] had

to control the thousands of chemical reactions, which would help the tiny bit of life move, assimilate food, and reproduce. In the most complicated organisms DNA had a more portentous role. Starting with a single, fertilized egg cell and moving through thousands of divisions, *DNA was to be responsible for mapping out the entire development of the individual.* The direction would start with the production of individual cells. In the individual cell, DNA was responsible for its thousand enzymes, their production and allocation. The right amount had to be produced at the right time and directed to the right place. The cells then had to be organized into tissues and the tissues integrated into organs and the organs merged into a functioning unit. Once the individual was complete, it had to be guided—again by DNA—into adulthood. And when the individual had been fully formed, DNA then faced a life time of work: repeated production of blood; replacement of cells; and always the production of the hormones, enzymes, and other materials that kept the individual functioning.

And to top it all, it had to be able to reproduce itself quickly and precisely.[52]

Suppose for a moment that a Creator went to that kind of incomparably intricate design just for His love of *mankind* (notice *that* word). Wouldn't you be overwhelmed with the realization of what *you* are?!

Consider one more example of DNA and the ineffable intricacy of its makeup: DNA has a code which geneticists are trying to break. Chemist Ernest Borek, saying that "the task of decoding DNA staggered even the bravest among us," illustrates the nature of the problem even when only one *invisible* bacterium is involved:

> We can make some quite accurate approximations on the number of different protein molecules in a cell; in turn we can estimate the minimum number of code letters of DNA needed to encompass all that information. Someone has calculated that for the storage of information for the proteins of the invisible colon bacillus . . . a closely typed book of 3000 pages would be needed.[53]

Dr. Beadle says that if the coded DNA instructions of a *single human* cell were put into English, "they would fill a 1000-volume encyclopedia."[54] Now consider this:

> Your personal DNA is peppered throughout your body in about 60 thousand *billion* specks—the average number of living cells in a human adult.[55]

That's 60,000,000,000,000 *volumes* of code for one adult human being. You can figure out the pages!

What does all this have to do with kinds? Just this:

> Above all . . . DNA must be faithful to itself. From generation to generation, it must copy itself exactly, insuring that mice give birth to mice, chickens to chickens, and rose bushes to rose bushes. . . .[56]

The geneticists we have read all agree on this role for DNA. Borek phrases it strongly:

> Every organism, however complex, contains in every one of its cells all the genetic information of that particular species.[57]

"In every cell . . . all the . . . information of that particular species. . . ." And kinds *cannot* breed out of their species, you will recall. So, if they must reproduce their own kind and each new member into the kind is loaded with DNA that will faithfully guarantee that he will remain in his kind, and grow up and perpetuate the process ad infinitum, then how could evolution have happened even once, not to mention the zillions of times it would have had to happen to get 1,200,000 species? How?

Author John Fried, who supplied the quote above about mice, chickens, and rose bushes, ponders the question for a few syllables and then gives an answer that is absolutely typical of evolutionists' responses to the big questions. He has just finished writing that DNA "must copy itself exactly, insuring that mice give birth to mice...." Then he says:

> Looking at it this way, it would seem that life's basic aim is to remain unchanged, to achieve, before anything else, a comfortable predictability. Yet this cannot be entirely true. For if DNA were really all that monotonous in its movement through time, all that perfect, unwilling and perhaps incapable of change, then the only form of life on earth today should be the direct and exact descendents of the very first DNA molecule whose home was the primordial sea....[58]

"Whose home was the primordial sea!" Who says so? Darwin, the holy one, of course. And all of his disciples. How did the sea get there? Accident. The air, sun, distance, balance, temperature? Accident. And how did something so complicatedly structured we can't even describe it come into being out of nonliving matter? Accident. And why did this thing evolve then when it doesn't evolve now? Accident. How did the first DNA molecule produce young not of its same kind? Accident.

And how did its supposed evolutionary offspring go against all genetic laws zillions of times and produce offspring of another kind? Accident.

We have a question that you may also have. How did all this incredible nonsense that passes under the label of science ever get such a hold on mankind? Accident....

One searches in vain for the causes of the remarkably solid and confident public image that evolutionary scientists have managed to project on the world at large. Notice this paragraph taken from *Ecological Genetics*—especially the last sentence and the mention of random drift:

> King and Jukes (1969), as well as Kimura (1968), have argued that evolution in DNA and proteins is largely due to selectively neutral mutations and random drift. Their view depends upon the supposition that some base pair changes in DNA do not result in the substitution of a different aminoacid into the encoded protein. That is to say, such mutations are "synonymous," because they do not alter the functions of the genes. *But if they do not alter the functions of the genes, they do not bring about evolution*[59] (our emphasis).

And, of course, we can't have something going on that doesn't bring about evolution! Simpson wrestles manfully with the genetic drift threat for several pages. Boldly he changes the calculations of the author of the concept (Sewall Wright) to fit his needs and proceeds with a verbal shell game which includes employing admitted guesses about natural selection, mutations, population unknowns, and genetic drift until he drops the subject with: "Nevertheless, it seems both possible and probable that drift has *sometimes* been involved [in origins of species]."[60]

It may be that the late respected geneticist, Richard Goldschmidt of the University of California, had the only way out for evolutionists. Since no other way could be found to escape the many dilemmas evolutionists faced in reconciling their theory with laws and facts, he proposed a unique answer to their problems. His solution? A big mutation; one that didn't accumulate gradually; one that violated all the gene theories; one that would be fatal if it had evolved.... It has been named "The Hopeful Monster."

And that is about where evolutionary "science" now rests!

But, speaking of monsters in relation to the lengths of which geneticists are being driven to get around the *kinds* question, the subject of *eugenics* bears mention.

Eugenics is "the science which deals with influences that improve inborn or hereditary qualities of a race or breed, especially of the human race."

It is really quite questionable whether eugenics would have gained the status it has if evolutionary thought had not come along. Certainly many practitioners of this branch of genetics give little or no thought to the question of the sacredness of human life. The founder of eugenics, by coincidence, was Charles Darwin's counsin, Francis Galton. (The little that we read about Galton, implies that he was a humane sort, and certainly not a salivating mad scientist that some eugenicists have been depicted as being. Yet he harbored some ideas that could easily be developed to fit the stereotype.) Author Macbeth reports:

> Sir Julian Huxley ... reports that Francis Galton (Darwin's cousin) and his disciple Karl Pearson, in the early days, applied mathematical methods of

extreme delicacy and ingenuity to the study of evolutionary problems.[61]

Galton—financially independent, interested in travel—used his leisure time to pursue the study of science and philosophy:

> His travels convinced him that man was much too much at the mercy of heredity. It would be better, he argued, if man could apply a rational breeding system to himself in order to perfect his kind.[62]

Galton suggested ways of improving the race by forbidding certain people—the insane, feeble-minded, confirmed criminals—the right to reproduce. Contrariwise, he would have encouraged capable young people to marry and reproduce by offering them money and recognition. His plans were not carried out in his day, and, although the idea has had many supporters over the years, it has basically not been practiced as Galton and other eugenicists might have wished.

The main reason, of course, is that:

> ... if it were to work at all, an all-out eugenics effort would entail a massive control over peoples' rights, a control few governments would try to implement. Furthermore, even a modest eugenics program involving government subsidies would take too long to really achieve positive genetic changes in man.[63]

Still, without government control or even participation, a certain number of human engineering experiments are usually in progress at a given time. Comic book type science fiction seems to be all too real in the minds of some eugenicists who would break certain genetic barriers and strive to replicate man in cloning experiments.*

Famed DNA scientist James Watson "has publicly demanded that Dr. Edwards abandon the Invit experiments" now proceeding in England.[65] Watson's demand stems from the fact that the Cambridge University's physiology lab is sponsoring an experiment which will implant a baby conceived outside the womb into

> ... the woman's receptive uterus ... by laparoscope. The mother-to-be will then go through the usual nine months of waiting ... and nature will have been by-passed in her most intimate and awesome act, conception.[66]

Obviously, this case involves human nature a great deal more than science (the husbands donate the sperm, the wives carry the child). Still, it is the implications of a *Brave New World* type genetic engineering that distresses many people.

And, make no mistake, people get *very* distressed when eugenicists begin toying with human beings in experimental ways. The public may have heard, or read a thousand times, that man is just another animal, but they don't believe it, and their views come out when scientists start messing too much with mankind.

But in a very real sense, the meager products that have resulted from efforts by eugenicists to alter human beings is all too clear proof that the law of like kinds could never have been broken in such a way as to make

---

*Cloning of frogs, where a replica of an individual is developed from one of its somatic cells, has already been successful. The technology for the cloning of mammals will be available within five years, and, unless research is stopped, the technology for the cloning of human beings might be available within anything from ten to twenty-five years.[64]

possible the evolution of all the varied forms of life on earth. With all their fine training, equipment, and intelligence, scientists are able to make only changes in variety of a species. And when they do come up with a useful hybrid, they give it good care and protection until it and others like it are mature and self-sufficient. Even their puny experiments require great amounts of time, equipment, organization, and design.

It is, of course, true that selective breeding under carefully controlled situations has greatly improved the quality of many plants and animals. But, as Dr. William J. Tinkle has pointed out, such improvements are only possible up to a certain point.

> The sugar beet was developed from the ordinary table beet by selecting for seed the ones with the highest sugar content. A hundred years of such selection in France increased the sugar content from 6 percent to 17 percent; but continued selection merely maintained the 17 percent and was unable to make greater gains. Such a result is to be expected.... Selection is a process of sorting among hereditary factors, not of changing them.[67]

The thought has occurred to us that eugenicists should reject evolution quicker than anyone, for they know firsthand that what they cannot do at this late date with all their sophisticated training and equipment, could never have happened in raw nature by accident.

Summary—Kinds

1. An inflexible law of genetics is that only like kinds can reproduce. This law would have had to have been broken zillions of times for evolution to have occurred.
2. Evolutionary scientists never face up to these deadly challenges to their childish myth. They have li-

braries full of double-talk on the subject. They have caused people to be afraid to challenge them, but *they are vulnerable* on every single thing they stand for.
3. DNA carries all the genetic information for the different species and has given *proof positive* that kinds cannot cross, and, therefore, that evolution could not have happened.
4. Evolutionary scientists must simply say that all the genetic rules were different "way back when. . . ." There is no basis for this assumption whatsoever; it is merely postulated to keep alive a theory that would die if the "doctors" left it on its own.
5. Eugenicists, geneticists who sometimes practice "human engineering," should know better than anyone the impossibility of accidental changes occurring to anything even remotely like the theory of evolution requires. They know that with all their organization, planning, and control they can really make only the most minor and limited changes.

Fossils

It should be emphasized that the fossil record is the *prime* source of so-called evidence for the general theory of evolution. It is of primary importance because it is interpreted as the record of what *has existed*, of what *has happened*. Many authorities agree that the decisive "evidence" for the general theory of evolution must be based upon what they consider to be historical. In other words, historical evidence for evolution must be found in the fossil record. Biologist Robert C. King pursued his work (as do other scientists) secure in the knowledge "that evolution . . . is unchallenged by thinking scientists," and that "the direct evidence for evolution comes from the fossil record as elucidated by paleontologists."[68] Charles Darwin and many other scientists since his time have proceeded on this assumption.[69]

What, then, do the fossils really tell us? Darwin himself was puzzled by the refusal of fossils to confirm his theory. In *The Origin of Species* he wrote:

> If the [evolution] theory be true, it is indisputable that before the lowest Cambrian stratum was deposited long periods elapsed, as long as, or probably far longer than, the whole interval from the Cambrian age to the present day; and that during these vast periods the world swarmed with living creatures.... To the question why we do not find rich fossiliferous deposits belonging to these assumed earliest periods prior to the Cambrian system, I can give no satisfactory answer.... The difficulty of assigning any good reason for the absence of vast piles of strata rich in fossils beneath the Cambrian system is very great.[70]

If the "difficulty" was very great when Darwin wrote his book that caused a revolution in man's thinking, matters had not improved over a hundred years later when in 1964 *The New York Times* reported:

> The chief puzzle in the record of life's history on earth: the sudden appearance, some 600 million years ago, of most basic divisions of the plant and animal kingdoms [sic]. There is virtually no record of how these divisions came about. Thus the entire first part of evolutionary history is missing.[71]

There is more evidence on this one point, but it all amounts to just another unexplainable and critical gap in the theory of evolution. The thing that is suspicious about this particular question (in case Darwin's remarks weren't clear) is that there are thick sediments below the

Cambrian deposits which should contain fossils of the Cambrian ancestors. But, unexplainably, there are no fossils. The *Scientific American* calls the appearance of animals in the Cambrian strata a "sudden event."[72] Darwin could "give no satisfactory reason" for this puncture in his theory; nor can anyone else.

While this great gap in the fossil record is serious enough by itself to make many discard Darwin's ideas, it is by no means the most serious flaw in the fossil evidence. The matter of missing links is even more damaging. Note what scientist John Moore says about the importance of links to the theory:

> The very essence of evolutionary thinking is slow change. Therefore a major prediction from the General Theory of Evolution would be that researchers would expect to find a record of *gradual transition* from the least complex to the complex. This is the major prediction from the general theory [of evolution]. In fact, if the General Theory of Evolution ever has any empirical basis, such a gradual transition of fossils *must* be found.
>
> In other words, systematic or regular gaps must be *absent* from the fossil record, and transitional forms at some stage between all phyla, classes, orders, families, genera, and species must be found. Such transitional forms must be found if the General Theory of Evolution, defined already as amoeba to man, has occurred. Of course, to be fair, one must admit that some sporadic gaps might be expected in the fossil record. The geological record is not complete. However, there must be *no regular or systematic gaps* in the fossil record.[73]

Since these transitional links must be found for the

evolution theory to meet the requirements of reason, logic, common sense, and science, it is fair to ask, "What does the fossil record show?"

The answer: No links. All who have looked have found that "a blank turns up where the common ancestor should be."[74] Garrett Hardin, in his book *Nature and Man's Fate* wrote on this problem:

> There was a time when the existing fossils of the horses seemed to indicate a straight-line evolution from small to large, from dog-like to horse-like, from animals with simple grinding teeth to animals with the complicated cusps of the modern horse. It looked straight-line—like the links of a chain. But not for long. As more fossils were uncovered, the chains played out into the usual phylogenetic net, and it was all too apparent that evolution had not been in a straight line at all, but that horses had now grown taller, now shorter with the passage of time.[75]

Alfred Wallace, whom you met earlier—the man who came up with the same theory as Darwin at approximately the same time—moved the example from horses to man. Noting that the distance between the brain of an ape was too incredibly far removed from the brain of the most primitive savage to justify calling the former a link in the evolutionary chain, you will remember that he wrote:

> Natural selection could only have endowed the savage with a brain a little superior to that of the ape, whereas he actually possesses one but very little inferior to that of the average member of our learned societies.[76]

Then as Macbeth further points out in his *Yale Review* article:

> Darwin realized that this was dangerous. He wrote to Wallace, "I hope you have not murdered too completely your own and my child."[77]

Again, more scientists could be quoted, but since there are no links there seems little reason to lengthen the list. The point is clear and telling: where there should be hundreds of millions of transitional links, *there are none.*

This fact cannot be overemphasized. There are clear-cut distinctions from specie to specie, both in the fossil record and in the study of contemporary species. If evolution occurred, there would be no such clear-cut distinctions. There would be instead a gradual connection more or less among all life. There would have to be billions and billions of fossil records of these gradual connections (links), and there would have to be millions upon millions of observable living links today. The truth is, however, that there is not one single fossil or one living example of a gradual connection. There is no missing link. Evolutionists lie or don't know the truth if they say otherwise.

So, if the whole Pre-Cambrian Missing Fossils Caper moved you a notch further toward realizing that evolutionists have been misleading the rest of us for over a century, then the fact that " . . . no intermediates have ever been observed . . . either in the present world or the fossil world"[78] should move you another notch. And once you start doubting the theory of evolution, the utter absurdity of it will magnify every day of your life. Your astonishment will be multiplied all the more as the full reach and scope of the theory in our world dawns on you. You will begin to see at least two important realities looming ahead for you and the entire world, both more promising perhaps than anything that has gone before, yet both facing obstacles. One reality you will see is that there have been and are now only two theories of how man got here, evolution and creation. When one is *proven* false—ludicrously false—then the other is ipso facto *proven* true. One of your realities, then, will be that a Master Planner, an ineffably loving and all-knowing Creator went to some pains to design you and all that can and cannot be seen. Each person will know how to deal with this reality when he fully recognizes and understands it. The second reality is that the message of evolutionary thought is deep in the bloodstream of the modern world. It is the raison d'être for the atheist-humanist approach to problem solving in economics, government, sociology, psychology, philosophy, the humanities, and other fields. This fact may awaken you as to how far the theory has penetrated into the thinking of modern people. And you will know that it must not be that way if man is to reject what is proven false and accept what is proven true. And you will know that there must be some way to get around all this entrenched power, held—*it must be remembered*—by well-intentioned good people, designed by a Creator just as all of us, and brought up believing what evolutionary scientists assured them was the factual truth.

Take a couple more examples from the fossil record: Most people know something about the Piltdown Man hoax. It is one of the very few examples that people in general know about which shows the gullibility, the childlike over-eagerness of the evolutionists to make their theory look scientific.

To those unfamiliar with the Piltdown hoax, the facts can be related very briefly in two parts. One part stresses the importance placed on the discovery of the "missing link," and can be appreciated from this encyclopedic account:

> The discovery which ranks next in importance . . . was made by Mr. Charles Dawson at Piltdown, Sussex, between the years 1911 and 1915. He found the greater part of the left half of a deeply mineralized human skull, also part of the right half; the right half of the lower jaw, damaged at certain parts but carrying the first and second molar teeth and the socket of the third molar or wisdom tooth. . . .
>
> Amongst British authorities there is now agreement that the skull and the jaw are parts of the same individual.[79]

The second part deals with the real nature of this badly needed "fossil link":

> One of the most famous fakes exposed by scientific proof was Piltdown Man, found in Sussex, England . . . and thought by some to be 500,000 years old. After much controversy, it turned out to be not a primitive man at all but a composite of a skull of modern man and the jawbone of an ape. . . . The jawbone had been "doctored" with bichromate of potash and iron to make it look mineralized.[80]

The teeth had even been filed to make them appear more authentic. The whole project was planned and executed by one, Mr. Charles Dawson. Can't you envision Dawson filing those teeth and doctoring the jawbone? A missing link! Wow! And, even though the curious Mr. Dawson died in 1916, "he did win fame in his own time as the fossil was named for him—Eoanthropus dawsoni"![81]

And the scientists put this impressive new evidence into books for two generations of school children to study and marvel at—and be convinced by—along with the other accumulating "facts."

We think there should have been a third part to the Piltdown hoax story; a part that, if it was tried at all, was ineffective. By this, we mean that the "scientists" who violated all the rules of scientific methods by pawning off on unsuspecting thousands this anti-intellectual fraud, should at least have printed retractions in other books. They should have at least been sent back to school. Or something! But when one is a priest in a new faith, then one's small errors are overlooked for the greater good of the faith, or so it seems.

There are other, less well-known cases about fossils that have the same earmarks as the Piltdown hoax. We will mention two: the Java Man fossils and the Neanderthal Man fossils.

Java Man has an important niche in the evolutionary theory's Hall of Fame. Hundreds of books and articles discuss him as a proven fact. Many books show a bust of his supposed likeness alongside Piltdown Man. Now and then Heidelberg Man is included. One high school world history textbook referred to the "Earliest Men: Peking, Java, and Heidelberg" in this not uncommon way in an introductory chapter:

> ... Early men were not handsome by our standards. They were short, squatty, and powerfully built. They had powerful jaws and sharply receding chins. Their foreheads were low, with heavy eyebrow ridges. In fact, scientists call Java Man Pithecanthropus erectus, which means something like "the man who looks like an ape and walks on his hind legs" ... no artifacts were found with Java Man.[82]

60

An earth science textbook shows the same busts—"Reconstructions of the facial features of three types of primitive man," and adds this information on Java Man:

> The brain of the specimen was larger than that of an ape, but several of his features were distinctly apelike. [It] ... was discovered on the island of Java in 1892, [and] is believed to be more than 500,000 years old.[83]

This text is typical in that it gives this view of such fossils:

> Thus, the fossil record supports the theory that all life is interrelated, and that the most complex forms have developed from the simple forms by a long series of gradual, evolutionary changes ... our knowledge ... is based primarily on fossils.[84]

So let us say that Java Man is a well-accepted and widely displayed example of fossil evidence validating the theory of evolution.

Then let us examine what is known about the blue ribbon fossil, Java Man.

A Dutch surgeon, Professor Dubois, collected the famous bone fragments with what might seem something less than great scientific care:

> The five fossil fragments found were: a skull cap which outwardly had the form which might be expected in a giant form of gibbon, a left thigh bone and three teeth. The most distant parts of the fragments were 20 paces apart. Later he added a sixth fragment—part of a lower jaw bone found in another part of the island but in a stratum of the same geological age.[85]

Speaking for ourselves, we find it a trifle unscientific to scrounge up a few pieces of bone here, a few pieces yards away, and then throw in another piece from a site four miles distant and call it "Java Man." It doesn't strengthen our faith in the good doctor to learn that he admitted that other bones of more recently deceased Javanese were in the same place where he made his discovery. Nor does it increase our trust to learn that Dubois published a monograph about his discovery in which he labeled his find the "intermediate form between the Anthropoids and Man," and furthered the theory of evolution by calling his find "the precursor of Man."[86] But then we were more perplexed than mistrustful to learn that

> Dubois became, as it were, his own opponent. Having discovered the earliest man, he fought doggedly throughout the rest of his life to maintain that *Pithecanthropus* was not an early man but a giant man-like ape.[87]

And this hodgepodge of duplicity and recantation is labeled "the first concrete proof that man has been subject to evolutionary change..."![88]

In addition to these strange doings about Java Man and Piltdown Man, the case of the much discussed Neanderthal Man gives us even graver doubts about the responsibility of evolutionary scientists.

Pierre Marcellin Boule drew a portrait of Neanderthal Man that depicted this supposed forerunner of modern man as a "stunted, beetle-browed creature who walked with bent knees and his arms dangling in front of him."[89] This concept by the respected French paleontologist "served as a model for several generations of artists and cartoonists."[90]

In other words, Boule, working from some bones that were unearthed around the time Darwin was causing a stir with his theory, gave us a model that is used in museums and books all over the world; a model accepted and perpetuated by other scientists; a model—as recent evidence indicates—that has served only to further evolutionary dogma and not the scientific truth.

The nature of the deception regarding Neanderthal fossils alone has several aspects, but one example will suffice here to make the point. The example to which we refer is the foisting of supposedly lifelike representations of supposedly pre-man types on the general public which thinks they are viewing scientific facts, when all they are really seeing is a figure who looks like what the evolutionary scientist wants him to look like!

Most of us learned that scientists could marvelously recreate just about anything, given a bone or two. A book on our shelves dated 1956 is typical in that it reinforced this common belief:

> It has been said that a good paleontologist could accurately reconstruct the entire skeleton of a fossil creature if he possessed a single tooth and a bone. Although this, of course, is an exaggeration yet it seems truly astounding that a scientist can completely restore a skeleton from only a small portion of its fossil remains.[91]

The fact, however, is that the skeleton is *not* what people in general and students in particular see. They see a creature with facial features and expressions calculated to give the impression that a lower man from whom we evolved is standing there with his knuckles on the ground looking like Boule drew him. But scientists can't tell what the eyes, ears, nose, and lips looked like. They don't know what the skin color was or the hair color or texture, whether there was a light or heavy beard or no beard. As the late Harvard anthropologist, Ernest

Hooton, honestly put it: "You can, with equal facility, model on a Neanderthal skull the features of a chimpanzee or the lineaments of a philosopher."[92]

(Check the Appendix under "Slime Hoax," pages 218-220, for another account of a hoax, not related to fossils, but enlightening about evolutionists.)

Have "scientists" ceased giving the world the impression that they know what so-called pre-man types looked like?

Hardly! We, as thousands of others, received in the mail very recently a colorful brochure from *Time-Life* announcing their new multi-volume set entitled: *The Emergence of Man*. One volume is called *The Missing Link* and has on its cover a "photopainting" of the long sought after missing link himself! Inside the brochure another "photopainting" depicts eight other "missing links" milling about in a grassy area with trees and a mountain in the background. The description below the very realistic looking "photopainting" points out that this is the way "Australopithecus [billed as the missing link between ape and man] looked two million years ago." The description proceeds:

> Leaving the forest for a hunting life in the savanna, Australopithecus was at first disorganized, with little family and group unity. About four and a half feet tall and 80 pounds, he was not the "hairy ape man" once supposed; recent studies have established that men and animals that hunt have little body hair. Though upright, Australopithecus walked with a slight stoop and carried his young on his back like his primate forebears.[93]

Think about each sentence for a minute—"Left the forest for a hunting life in the savanna...." How could anyone make that statement with such apparent certainty?! Was a note found in the forest saying—"Have gone to the savanna for hunting"? or a note found in the savanna saying, "Have left forest to hunt here"? How marvelous that "scientists" can know from a few pieces of bone or whatever they found that those missing links were "at first disorganized [at first!], with little family or group unity." How, *how* can they make that generalization? Height? Weight? Maybe, but appearance? Impossible. But at least we've gotten rid of the "hairy ape man" after four generations of seeing him represented as scientific truth!

We wonder what happened to the old evolutionist adaptation idea when we learn that "recent studies have established that men and animals that hunt have little body hair." Or is this just in warm climates? And how can you tell about hair from bones? And what did the missing links find that was so tasty in the savanna that they left a forest where so many edible animals make their homes? "Walked with a slight stoop?" Why not; that makes him closer to the apes, right? " . . . and carried his young on his back like his primate forebears. . . ." This one stumps our panel of experts, folks! The panel wants to know just how anyone could make that assumption! Carried their young on their backs. . . .

Two thousand years is a long time. Two million years is a *thousand* times two thousand. Was there a forest and a savanna there then? What about the ice age? Yet the advertisement assures us that the new series "tells the story of man's beginning *as it really was*. . . ." (their emphasis!) "You don't just *read* this new information—you *see* it."[94] The first volume, just off the press, "is an important first step to understanding where we have come from, and how we may be evolving." A pictorial chart next to this book advertisement shows "The Face from Fish to Man" and starts with a shark's head and ends up with a man's head—just like that. Nobody has noticed any of the in-between animals they show (lizards, opossums, lemurs, monkeys, gorillas) changing into anything else, nor has there ever been a *single* fossil found to substantiate such an unscientific and childishly fanciful deduction. But there they are and backed up by *Time-Life!*

But this sort of irresponsibility does not seem to disturb anyone at *Time-Life* or in their stable of "scientists." The photographs are superb; the drawings convincing; the blurbs fetchingly worded; the price reasonable. They will sell. Many will get a prominent spot in the neighborhood school library. If evolution is in the textbooks and in *Time-Life* sponsored books, it's got to be fact. . . .

Any twelve-year-old kid knows that. Of course, the kids' parents may insist now and then that there is another story of how man got here. But it's kind of an unscientific sounding story and it isn't supported by "photopaintings" and real pictures of sharks and monkeys; nor is it supported by such respectably titled scientists, selflessly saving mankind from stupid myths. Even the parents begin to wobble and, together, we proceed to prod civilization into an intellectual muck that is already succeeding in making problems unsolvable and lives hopeless.

Before going on to another category of evidence against evolution, we, the authors, ask you to read another paragraph from the brochure, this one on the front and embellished with color photographs of the sea at dawn, several kinds of animals, lightning against a blue-black sky, and an artist's concept of a prehistoric man. If you read it very carefully, as we did, you will find at least a dozen assumptions incapable of being supported by one shred of evidence.

If yours is a faith in evolution that has grown deep over the years, carefully nurtured and fortified by a pseudoscientific clergy from the academic world, then try to read even more carefully....

> Out of the water came life, perhaps first fired by a lightning stroke. Primitive matter on the edge of existence, it slowly evolved into cells and simple organisms that swam in those ancient seas and ponds. Eons later fish appeared, and the thrust of evolution shaped a few that could live both on land and sea, as Asian mudskippers do today. Some abandoned the sea entirely and became reptiles that grew and flourished. Dinosaurs, many 10 times as big as elephants, took over the land. Among them scurried little furry creatures — the first mammals. Some of them, like the modern loris from Laos, took to the trees; among these animals, man finds his forebears. For it was from the trees that something swung down to the green earth again and took the first steps that led to The Emergence of Man.[95]

Isn't that an interesting yarn? It's well-written, certainly, and if you didn't know that it was based *entirely* on assumptions, you could even take it seriously. The same thing can be said about fossil "evidence," obviously, and for all of evolution theory as well. One is led to wonder how matters would have developed if scientists such as Cuvier, Agassiz, Blyth, and others who rejected evolutionary explanations had prevailed instead of Darwin, Spencer, Huxley, and others. Georges Cuvier, for example, the "father of paleontology," a man who knew "more about ... comparative vertebrate anatomy than anyone in Europe," said straightaway, "Fossil Man does not exist." All the efforts to prove him wrong over these many years have failed. Professor Leakey's lifetime efforts to find the missing link had come to naught when he died on October 1, 1972. An article about those efforts spoke of how his "enthusiasm led him to premature conclusions," and that "more intensive study of *Homo Hablis* [his main find] throws considerable doubt on the distinctive character assigned to it by Leakey."[96] Thus, after over a century of effort, Cuvier's statement "Fossil Man does not exist" remains valid. And as long as scientists look for the evolutionary forerunner of man, they will fail. They can't find what couldn't have existed. And if evolutionists can't hold their theory together for any of the other animals, they certainly cannot make it apply to man, the most complex of all creatures. The question of how modern man "could have appeared so suddenly without known antecedents anywhere" has not been solved and will not be solved from the "fossil record."[97] "Missing links," writes Lincoln Garrett, "will always evade and challenge man's imagination."[98]

Summary—Fossils

1. Although it is the prime source of so-called evidence for evolution, the fossil record contains *not one single* piece of verified evidence indicating evolving fossils.
2. Darwin could give no satisfactory answer as to why there are no fossils in the pre-Cambrian strata of the earth. Since evolutionary theory demands "ancestors" for the fossils that are found, and since there are none, "Darwin's Dilemma" is just as deadly to his theory today as it ever was.
3. Piltdown Man, hailed as a missing link, fooled "scientists" for forty years, though it was no more than

a few bones carefully treated and put in a place where they would be found.
4. Java Man, called "the first concrete proof that man has been subject to evolutionary change," is revealed to be just an ape.
5. The picture that *you* have in your mind of prehistoric ape-men is the result of artists' concepts that fulfill the evolutionists' needs. There is *no way* scientists can describe from their bones how these decidedly *un*human creatures actually looked. They simply deceive when they say otherwise.
6. The assertions by a new series from *Time-Life* about what new fossil finds in Australia prove is a perfect example of unscientific assumptions presented as fact. Everybody, but particularly parents of school-age children, have a right to demand scientific honesty on this issue and all similar ones that influence a child's view of life.
7. The fossil record provides only damaging evidence *against* evolution; it provides no evidence to support the theory.

But let us turn now to some matters related to time, the veil that shy evolutionists must wear when they come into contact with those outside the faith. . . .

Time

Time, as poets and insurance salesmen remind us, is the enemy of life. But time has its friends too. Without great, incomprehensible, immeasurable stretches of time to fall back on, the evolutionists would be sitting ducks for the barbed queries of even high school students. *Time* is the evolutionists' refuge from the slings and arrows of logic, scientific evidence, common sense, and the multiplication table. When Lord Kevin, the renowned physicist, calculated that the earth was only thirty million or so years old, Darwin labeled him an "odious specter" and said: "I am greatly troubled at the short duration of the world according to Lord Kevin, for I require for my theoretical views a very long period."[99]

And so have all evolutionists since then.... In a recent work by a well-known American biologist and doomsdayist, we read:

> *In view of the time available* [our emphasis] for the evolutionary process, mutation, recombination, selection, and drift quite adequately account for the diversity of life.[100]

Dr. Paul Henshaw, a prolific and able writer who grounds his work on the evolutionary theory, supplies for us a standard time lapse used by many scientists. In *This Side of Yesterday* he notes:

> Indications are that the earth formed a hard crust and oceans four to five billion years ago ... and that the biologic cells came into existence one or two billion years thereafter. On the basis of data as given and of identification of the human species as now defined, man then came into existence during or shortly before the Pleistocene Epoch* which began about a million years ago and extended to about ten thousand years ago.[102]

In the story of evolution—or "spontaneous generation," as he argued it should be called—George Wald says, "Time is the hero of the plot."[103]

And so it is—or the villain as it may turn out for the evolutionists.... In an action manual a whole roster of

---

*One has a choice on how far back the Pleistocene Epoch was. *Columbia Encyclopedia* states that the Pleistocene Age began "500,000 to 1,000,000 years ago (depending on the geological time scale employed)."[101]

antievolutionary scientists have a number of things to say about *time* in relation to the earth and the theory of evolution. This is one statement of theirs relevant to the pseudoscientific, publicly misleading dating methods used:

> ... former methods of dating the age of the earth are now regarded as obsolete and have been superseded by methods based on the radio-activity of elements found in the crust of the earth. These methods all depend on a "known" amount of radio-active element being sealed up in a rock, "undisturbed," and decaying at a "regular" rate. The "known" amount and the "regular" rate cannot be verified. They are assumed. Also, geochemists point out that it is the *exception* rather than the rule for elements to exist "undisturbed." Therefore, giving any specific age to the earth is hypothetical and should not be taught without definite qualifying statements showing their limitations.[104]

The proven uncertainties about scientific dating are a well-kept secret. The average person reading his newspaper or magazine gets the clear impression that dating is a science as exact as the addition of fractions. This recent UPI release from London is typical:

> For 167 million years dinosaurs dominated the world of the beasts and then mysteriously vanished from the earth.[105]

Not 150 or 175, but *167* million! That seems rather exact, doesn't it? Mr. Baker (the scientist behind the 167 million figure) gets this penchant for unverifiable exactness honestly, though. In fact, the practice seems to form part of the particular habit of mind that characterizes the evolutionist, who makes up for his lack of evidence and proof with a show of unquestionable exactitude. A hundred years ago the same approach was just as evident. In explaining the length of time needed for a gradual cooling of the earth so that evolution could get moving, Sir William Thompson calculated that the process took some 98 million years, but Darwin found this figure too small and too rounded. Southall notes that: "Mr. Darwin represents that it must have taken three hundred and six million six hundred and sixty-two thousand four hundred years."[106]

One problem with uncovering such claims to exactness, we have found, is that one becomes unconvinced by even well-established and accepted measurements that probably can be proven but are given as if there were no difficulties in such calculations. Take 186,000 miles per second, the speed of light, for example. Seven and a half times around the earth in the snap of a finger is pretty fast. How does one start and stop any kind of measuring or recording device without losing some fraction of a second which would cause substantial error? Well, it can be done, and by more than one method apparently. So we must assume that some of what the scientists are giving out as fact is actually verifiable. But the methods of dating prehistoric evidence are so far removed from the speed-of-light-kind of exactness that they don't deserve the label "scientific"!

Brilliant but stubborn Ernst Mayr can lead us into another aspect of time with his insightful observation:

> A new conceptual danger to the evolutionary theory at the present time comes not from metaphysics but from physics. . . . Those who try to explain the pathway of evolution in terms of the

laws of physics do not seem to realize how dangerously close they sail to preformism.[107]*

One can see why evolutionists are unnerved at the encroachment of scientific laws from physics. These are demonstrable, verifiable laws as opposed to the rarefied guesswork employed by evolutionists and hence are a threat to their position.

Let us look at the two laws of thermodynamics. The First Law—the Law of Conservation of Energy—says that nothing is being created or destroyed now. Energy (everything, basically) is being transformed into something else. It looses some heat or energy when transformed into something else. If creation is not taking place now, evolution must have stopped for some unexplained reason. Go back five thousand years, or ten thousand, or as far as you can imagine (or even as far as evolutionists can imagine!). Do you think the First Law of Thermodynamics was different in those times? Then keep in mind that this unbendable Law of Physics had to be different "then" or evolution couldn't have occurred, because if it were the same, nothing could have been created or destroyed ... except by You Know Who. Take your pick: Myth based on a violation of the First Law of Thermodynamics ... or Creation!†

Preformism: An old theory that every germ cell contained the organism of its kind fully formed, and that development consisted merely in increase in size.

†It is a major contradiction too, you will note, to have evolutionists arguing that conditions must have been and had to be *different* when life started to evolve. Then in another breath, they say those same conditions must have been and had to be the *same* as they are now for the dating methods to be valid.

Still, evolutionists tend to have a very strong faith in their fairy tale about the origin of the species. Many, despite the overwhelming scientific and logical case to the contrary, will continue weaving strange tales about how—if you allowed enough time—an amoeba could have evolved into Sergi Rachmaninoff. Even after you have thrown the First Law of Thermodynamics at them, many hold their ground. It is not easy to overthrow a belief, however absurd and harmful it may be, which your civilization has promulgated as the scientific truth for the better part of a century!

But, no matter, the Second Law of Thermodynamics is just as deadly to the evolution theory as the First Law. Since it too involves time and *time* is the main crutch of the evolutionists after their other arguments are exposed, let us kick it once more to be sure.

The Second Law says that time causes decay. This is not difficult to understand. Every material thing that is within our experience verifies the Second Law. Houses decay, trees decay, people decay. Even pyramids decay, their inhabitants' wishes notwithstanding. Since things decay with time, it follows that: we are in a more decayed world now than before; that is, the Law says that things don't evolve (develop), they deteriorate and decay. If *nothing* can be shown to be improving (evolving), and it is also true that *nothing* can be shown to be *devolving* (going backwards), then the Second Law must surely put the pistol to the head of the dying evolutionist.

However, let's leave the argument from physics and approach the issue another way. The issue is this: Arguments for evolution can be beaten down by scientific facts to the point that no rational person would base his life on such odds.* But the "scientists" maintain that given enough time the impossible would become possible. Since no one can envision even ten thousand years—much less a half-million or a million years—"scientists" can hide behind the two thousand millions of years that they say evolution took, and they can hide there in relative safety. They think!

It is fascinating to observe how Professor George Gaylord Simpson sweats and heaves to compress evolution into the period called for by the mythmakers. Certainly he knows full well the need for great lengths of time to lend *any* credibility to the theory of evolution. Yet, we perceive that—even allowing for his completely unfounded and arbitrary assumptions—he reveals two classic flaws in the evolutionist's time machine. See what you think:

He notes that the

> morphological difference [something you can see] between modern opossums and some Cretaceous opossums is slight [there is *no* difference], but some 60 million years of evolution occurred between them. If the missing pre-Cretaceous sequence changed at a comparable rate, transition from a reptile to an opossum can hardly have taken less than 600 million years; it probably took several times that long.

Of course he says all this is absurd, that when you

---

*If you had one chance in ten you might bet on a horse race. One chance in a million is ridiculous, but you might bet in a lottery or something. One in a billion; never. One in a trillion; be serious! But evolutionists not only want you to bet on a number that is followed by at least thousands of 500-page volumes full of zeros, they also want you to agree that *that* is the way it happened because it couldn't have been the other way!

take actual cases and estimate *backward* in time you simply don't have enough time to get much more done in two billion years than to get from a reptile to an opossum! And two billion years is how long evolutionists say it took all life to evolve! Therefore, evolution couldn't be, so naturally the technique is absurd. The bat's wing gave him the same problem. He wrote:

> ... if a structural unit, such as a bat's wing, be studied, it may be found [it *is* found] that its recorded rate of evolution is effectively zero. The bat's wing has not essentially progressed since the middle Eocene.... Extrapolation of this rate in an endeavor to estimate the time of origin from a normal mammalian manus [wing, hand?] might set that date before the origin of the earth.[108]

This is a serious problem for evolutionists, we think you will agree. The evidence that we do have simply tells us what DNA and everything else tells us, viz., species don't evolve from other species. The extinct ones are just extinct. There is no evidence that they evolved from anything or into anything else. But on the *time* problem which is very serious, how does Simpson get out of the dilemma? Watch!

He says we can get "some idea of probable rates of evolution ... by comparing the possible lengths of the gaps ... of the relatively continuous record ... for which there is fair knowledge. These estimates are highly unreliable because ... of personal opinion ... and [the fact that] no objective method of measurement exists as yet." From this mushy, unscientific premise he concludes that "the estimates of lengths of unknown origin sequences ... has taken place in less ... than a third of the time involved in later spread and diversification."[109]

So, abracadabra! and the time is reduced by two-thirds. But even that is much too long for the evolutionists' needs. Thus, "in spite of these uncertainties and unavoidable inaccuracies," he guesses that " . . . faster rates of evolution . . . had to go on . . . possibly ten or fifteen times as fast. . . ."[110] (Accelerated evolution when you need it! Isn't scientific proof wonderful?!)

One more thing here on *time*. . . . Notice this harmless sounding thought a few pages after the above: " . . . the transitional populations do not necessarily, or even probably, occur in the same spot throughout the millions of years involved in a major transition."[111] (*Transition* means "evolution.") We have two questions, one about the geography and one about the time involved. 1) If you find something in a certain spot and it probably didn't evolve there, how do you know that what you found evolved from something else? 2) If it takes millions of years to carry off a major transition (remember the opossum), and *man* is a major transition (the most major of all!), how could he have evolved in the mere one or two million years allotted to him by evolutionists? Time indeed is the hero of the evolutionists' plot!

But we doubt that there is any refuge for evolutionists anywhere—even behind a mist of two thousand million years!—once Truth picks up their scent. Hence—though no further evidence than has already been presented need be advanced to give the lie to the evolution theory—it is instructive to have a passing look at least at the highly questionable methods used to estimate those long periods of time that shield evolutionists from a critical evaluation of their theory.

First, let us take one more notice of the fact that vast, incomprehensible periods of *time* have been a necessary precondition for the evolution theory from its earliest days. Hotton records that "Darwin once confessed that his books 'came out of Sir Charles Lyell's brain' " and that:

> What Lyell had given the great evolutionist was a new geologic time scale, without which, Darwinian scholar, Loren C. Eiseley contends, "there would have been no *Origin of Species.*"[112]

The dating methods of Darwin's day were not as scientifically sophisticated, of course, as they are now. Yet Darwin was not shy about making judgments on the number of millions of years this or that development required (you will recall the length of time he gave the earth to cool was 306,662,400 years!).

But a few examples from the *modern* techniques for dating can be just as instructive as Darwin's mad guess. Accordingly, let us examine briefly a few of the dating techniques presently in use. We can begin with *carbon 14*. This is the one most people have heard about. It sounds scientific, and it is. The only thing most people don't hear about are its severe limitations, unaccountable inconsistencies, and baffling "wobble." Nevertheless, it is the workhorse of the dating techniques and is considered "useful in determining carbonaceous material younger than 30,000 years. It has a half-life of 5700 years."[113] (Most sources say 50,000 years and 5600 years, but such discrepancies—though common—are minor in the business of estimating time in the past.)

The idea is to measure the amount of radioactive carbon 14 left in a bone or some other find and determine how long ago the animal lived or the flint axe was chipped, or whatever. The most obvious limitation of carbon 14 is its admitted inability to reach back more than thirty thousand years (and this figure is challenged by many scientists who say eight thousand or ten thousand is more like it). And even thirty thousand years is not the batting of an eyelash compared to the time needed by evolutionists. Anyway, that shortcoming is admitted. But the unaccountable inconsistencies, and the enigmatic wobble we mentioned tell us something useful also about the caliber of this important weapon in the evolutionists' arsenal.

Three paragraphs in the July 1970, *Scientific American* describe the inconsistencies and the wobble of which C14 is guilty. (See Appendix—"The Bristlecone Correction"—for a full statement.) For some time, the article notes, students of ancient history have been puzzled by the discrepancies between known historical dates (First Egyptian Dynasty, etc.) and the ages assigned to these same items by C14. Certain evergreen trees in central California date back over seven thousand years—and have rings in the wood to prove it. When C14 is applied to these rings, however, a peculiar thing happens in that "the carbon 14 underestimation of age increases with the increase in the true age of the specimen."[114] Other checks confirm this tendency to increased discrepancy with age, and must raise the serious question as to whether this tendency might not well accelerate with still increased age to the point that C14 has a very limited usefulness indeed.

But the "wobble" raises even more serious doubts, the *most* serious of which seem to have been overlooked in this very article! Students have found a "wobble" that always comes up when they examine tree rings that were formed in the sixteenth and seventeenth centuries. " . . . tree rings that were formed in 1520 and 1640 both yield the same date: 1570."[115] Other studies show

> . . . similar wobbles; there are several between 1800 and 2500 B.C. and earlier ones around 3000

and 3600 B.C. The causes of the underestimation and the wobbles are not yet understood.[116]

We would ask the reader to notice two important observations that could have been made about this one experiment that do serious damage to the C14 dating technique. One: If several wobbles are observable back to 3600 B.C. (as far as written records go), then what would give us any confidence that further wobbles or even *super* wobbles don't occur when C14 is used to test even older samples? Obviously, the confidence factor and hence the scientific factor is sadly lacking here—which is all right, of course, if that's all that can be done. But, scientists, please don't pretend you know things accurately on the basis of C14 tests back thirty or fifty thousand years! You don't!

Two: The discrepancies *usually* showed C14 results indicating a younger age, and the last sentence of the article mentions that neither the causes of these *under*estimations nor the wobble is understood. But the wobble also contains an *over*estimation error! One tree ring that was known to date from 1640 showed 1570 under C14 testing. That's older by 70 years. And 70 years out of the 330 years since 1640 is over a 20 percent error on even that short period! How much justification is there for calling such an erratic and *unknown* technique as this "scientific"?

About as much as the others. Consider these new dating marvels: *Science* magazine for June 5, 1970, ran an article by Andre Boudin and Sara Deutsch entitled: "Geochronology: Recent Development in the Lutetium-176/Hafnium-176 Dating Method." The evidence was presented and it was formidable appearing to one unversed in these arcane matters. But something did stand out:

> For Lu concentration (Lutetium-176), the precision is 3.5 percent. . . . The precision for Hf measurement (Hafnium-176) is no better than 10 percent. . . .[117]

So the probability of error is 96.5 percent in the case of Lu-176 and 90 percent for Hf-176. Very impressive scientific technique, we thought. *Fission Track Ages* is another dating technique. In this example four authors put together two pages in *Science* for April 17, 1970, and titled their work: "Fission Track Ages and Ages of Deposition of Deep-Sea Microtektites." One of the highlights of this study pointed out that:

> Potassium/argon ages of ash layers . . . indicate that the microtektites . . . were deposited about 1.2 million years ago rather than 0.7 million years ago as suggested by the magnetic stratigraphy.[118]

Now, how are you going to feel when you go along basing your life on the 0.7 million year figure suggested by the magnetic stratigraphy, and then, all of a sudden potassium/argon comes into the picture and you have to increase everything by 500,000 years? Or 5/7? Or 71 percent? Messes up your whole day, doesn't it? Well, don't let it; that is about average for the "science" of prehistoric dating.

But, potassium/argon is one of the heavyweights in the dating business and deserves closer scrutiny.

Potassium/Argon

Actually, two other dating "clocks" can be lumped in with potassium/argon for our purposes here. They are uranium-lead, and rubidium-strontium. The chief characteristic of all three is that they "can be used only to measure vast periods of time, ranging from hundreds of millions to billions of years."[119] And those are the kinds of estimates that evolutionists cherish. For, remember:

> To the geologists, time is what space is to the astronomer—vastness beyond the thoughts of people ... enough to make "all things possible."[120]

The *half-life* of potassium-argon is usually listed at 1.3 *billion* years. The half-life for Uranium 238-Lead 206 is 4.5 *billion* years; for Rubidium-Strontium it is 47.0 *billion* years. Some idea of what is supposed to be happening to produce these silly numbers may be seen with cobalt-60 which has a half-life of 5.3 years (that's right, not billion or million, just years). If you had a 1-ounce block of cobalt-60 and let it decay for 5.3 years, you would have 1/2 ounce. The next 5.3 years would leave you with 1/4 ounce. You would have 1/8 of an ounce after 15.9 years, and so on. With potassium/argon, you start with an ounce and wait a mere 1.3 billion years and you will see that you have only 1/2 ounce left. How much would you lose in some reasonable length of time such as five years? 5/1,300,000,000, naturally. And could this be measured accurately, you inquire? Scientists assure us it can; not by weight, of course, but by detecting the number of atoms in a hundred million or so that will change every year. We called a physical scientist at a local university. "How can such time spans be measured?" we asked. "What kinds of instruments could these possibly be that could know how much argon was in a specimen, or how could you tell in a month or a year that something was aging on a *billion* year gauge?"

"I don't know. I have no idea," he replied quite forthrightly.

We are not the only skeptics. Henry Faul, an authority on dating techniques, has his doubts too:

> It is difficult to be certain whether a significant amount of environmental argon was originally enclosed in any K-Ar (potassium-argon) system used for age determination because there is no basis for estimating the isotopic composition of original argon.[121]

It may be of some use. We have our doubts, a pattern that develops when one begins checking into the "scientific" evidence surrounding *any* phase of the evolutionary theory! So it is too with the fluorine dating technique.

Fluorine Analysis

Used with good results on the Piltdown hoax, the fluorine test still leaves much to be desired. This is so because

> ... the amount of fluorine taken up also depends, of course, on the amount of fluorine in the soil. If the latter is rich in fluorine, any bodies imbedded in it may become so rapidly saturated that a fluorine analysis is of little use in estimating its age. It must be emphasized, therefore, that the analysis permits an estimation only of the *relative* antiquity of fossil material from the same deposit. Thus it does not permit a comparison of the relative (or the absolute) antiquity of fossilized bones derived from different deposits in which the fluorine content of the soil may vary widely.[122]

An interesting application of this less-than-first-rate dating technique can be seen when, according to Bowen, the

> ... human thigh-bones found near Trinil, Java ... were proved to be contemporary with the skull of Java man by applying the fluorine technique. While this does not prove that the bones came from the same individual, it does show that they came from men living at the same time.[123]

This is a very curious comment when we know from Dr. Dubois's own words (see p. 62) that he, the discoverer of Java man, insisted that his find was an ape, not a man, and now we find that the fluorine analysis shows that *men* lived at the same time. Must one conclude that an ape was buried in the human graveyard? Or that a lot of Javanese were buried in an ape graveyard? Or is the fluorine analysis—good only for remains of low antiquity at best, and then in some very qualified ways—just another weak measuring device with a ring of scientific accuracy about it?

We must confess that this is exactly the impression the evidence gives us. For all their claims and esoteric labels, it appears very much as though scientists are still using stone axes of a sort to measure the age of other stone axes.

There comes a point when the question of life arising through the evolutionary process changes from improbable to impossible. That point can be reached by not one but by several routes, as we have demonstrated and could continue to demonstrate. All that is being done now is to raise "impossible" to a level so that not even the most wild-eyed, salivating evolutionist could ask for more. Even seeking refuge in unlimited time won't work. It too is a leaky boat.

But exposing the highly erratic, scientifically flabby dating techniques employed is by no means the only way to fill this sinking boat with still more holes. Among others working on the subject, scientists at the Creation Science Research Center have organized many of these antievolutionary evidences in a well-documented and persuasive manner.[124] Through a variety of novel dating methods (comets, lunar soil analysis, population extrapolations, volcanic activity, new interpretations of the Geologic Column, and others) this Center represents one of several attempts now in motion to bring the high priests of evolution down from their ivory towers to do battle.

We applaud their efforts. The first order of business, it seems to us, is to get the evolutionists' deeply entrenched guesswork out in the sunshine of objective scrutiny. There it will wither and die, thereby touching off an antievolutionary revolution in man's thinking.

Accordingly, from this point on, we prefer to leave behind the purely scientific arguments against evolution, and to proceed instead with a number of logical, commonsense reasons for throwing out evolutionary theory, and for starting to recognize the scope of the wonderment that settles upon one when he considers the life and the earth about him as an act of special creation.

Summary—Time

1. Vast, incomprehensible periods of time provide a ready refuge for evolutionary theorists. When critics begin to bark at them too threateningly, they get in their time machines and go back two and even three billion years where all things were possible.... Time is the hero of the evolutionary plot.
2. Evolutionists give the impression that they can ac-

curately date various things going back hundreds of millions of years. The truth that no one hears is that these time measurements are all made on the basis of assumptions which violate not only common sense but the First and Second Laws of Thermodynamics as well.

3. The evolutionists thought they had enough time to shield their theory from any attack, but with the gradual wearing away of the main supports of the theory, i.e., mutations, natural selection, the inflexibility of genetic laws, the nonexistent fossil evidence, etc., the thing that has happened is that one can prove mathematically that no amount of time—much less a mere two billion years—will suffice for evolution.

4. The C14 dating technique has limitations which virtually remove it as an evolutionist's tool. Other radioactive dating techniques can not justifiably be called scientific, unless "scientific" is expanded to cover unreasonable assumptions and margins of error running to over 90 percent.

Part Three

THE LOGIC OF SPECIAL DESIGN AND CREATION

What Is Logical?

As with virtually all basically simple concepts the idea of *logic* has been made into a complicated mental exercise requiring specialists and experts to comprehend it. This practice has done little to accommodate the needs of people. Accordingly, the attempt here will be to pose questions and state facts and relate stories which will by their very nature suggest one conclusion. Anyone able to think at all can understand logic. All that is required is to make certain that whatever a person concludes is inevitable, if he has reasoned consistently and correctly, and could be concluded no other way. That, we think, is what logic really is, what we shall treat it as, and what we shall propose that it be.

For a start, we would ask you to focus your attention on any man-made object. It doesn't matter how simple or how complicated it may be. It may be a ring on your finger, your front door, a child's toy, or a telephone. Anything will do. Ask yourself a question to which you already know the answer, that is, was this object planned and made? Ask this about any man-made object and ask it for the rest of your life and the answer will always be the same: Yes, it was planned and made. That is logical. That is fact.

Now ask yourself another question to which you already have a logical, factual answer, namely, is there any man-made object that has *any* part of itself that did not originally come from something that is already present in the natural world around us? It all came from there? You are sure? Is that a fact? Is it logical? Would it be illogical and nonfactual to say the object came from nothing? Would it also be illogical and nonfactual to say that the object (pencil, door, airplane) just happened to take its present form by accident, without planning? If you agree such things cannot happen, then you know—without special training in logic or mathematical equations—you *know* what is illogical and what is not.

So far, then, you *know* (as opposed to feel or have blind faith in) that all man-made objects required planning and that they are made from materials in the world around us.

Using the logical mind that you have—that *all* of us have—ask yourself if there is anything in the world of nature (the world around us) that is man-made. There isn't any such thing, you say? (We knew you would say that because it's logical.) But tell us now if there are or are not thousands (millions, billions) of things in the nonman-made world. There are? You know for a fact there are, don't you? There are thousands of kinds of plants, you say; there are thousands of kinds of animals (there are 100,000 species of moths alone); there are many elements, etc.? You are certain? You are positive? It is a fact?

Then let us repeat what we are sure of beyond logical question so far:

1. All man-made objects require planning;
2. All man-made objects are made from materials in the world around us;

3. There is nothing in the world of nature (the non-man-made world) that was made by man;
4. There are thousands (millions, billions) of actual nonman-made things in the world.

Now let us think about the word *simple* and the word *complex*. A child can make a mud pie. A certain amount of planning is required, but not much. It is a simple creation. That same child years later may design a computer or build a house or bake a real pie. These activities require more planning. They are complex creations. So, let us add another number to our list of logical facts:

5. Man can plan and create simple and complex works.

Now let us look at the natural nonman-made world and again think of *simple* and *complex*.

Let us consider the simplest of all forms of life around us, that is, the one-celled animal. This is a microscopic cell about one-thousandth of an inch long. That is a fact. How simple is the cell? A Cambridge University professor of zoology, Sir James Gray, says:

> A bacterium is far more complex than any inanimate system known to man. There is not a laboratory in the world which can compete with the biochemical activity of the smallest living organism.[1]

Another source tells us that

> to grasp in detail the physico-chemical organization of the simplest cell is beyond our capacity.[2]

"The cell is as complicated as New York City,"[3] another observer notes. It is more complicated than any computer man has made. It is complicated and small to be sure; but consider this for complexity and smallness:

> The infinitesimal size of the nuclei can be realized

89

when it is estimated that one million times one million could fit inside the average atom.[4]

Yet the cell is the *simplest* form of life, a nonman-made "thing." With your permission, we will state this as a fact:

6. The most simple thing in living matter is more complicated than the most complicated man-made thing.

And, of course, one shouldn't forget that whether he makes a mud pie or a computer, man must plan and then use materials which he did not and cannot create out of nothing.

Now, let us look at something complicated in the nonman-made world. Let us consider you, or, to leave out the "simple" parts of you, just your brain.

Your brain has ten billion (ten thousand million) of those "simple" type cells in it. Each one is more complex than the London telephone system, keep in mind, and be reminded too that man has not and will not create even this "simplest" life form without using "ingredients" which he did not make; nor has he or will he ever create even this "simplest" life form without doing considerable planning in his laboratory.

Your ten-billion-cell brain is too complicated to describe in words. "Complicated" though our languages may be, there are not enough words, there is not enough paper, not enough ink to detail the ineffable complexity of the brain. It has not been done. It will not be done. That is a logical fact.

7. Many nonman-made things—the human brain, for example—are too complex for man to describe, much less plan and create.

One could go on *forever* making these kinds of examples, but we have enough facts to raise a few questions and provide logical answers to them.

If man's most complex creations (which require years, even generations of planning) are less complex than the least complex nonman-made life form, does this make the logical side of you wonder if there is a Designer, a Creator? Is it logical to you that one could put into a big box all the components of such a simple manmade object as a motorcycle (gears, electrical system, mirror, bolts, paint, etc.) and shake it, or leave it in the sun and rain, or put it under water for a million years—is it logical that a finished motorcycle would result? You *know* logically, that it wouldn't happen, but does this help you to realize that nothing even as simple as a motorcycle can achieve order, structure, functionality by accident? Consider this statement by the distinguished British biologist, Woodger:

> Unstable organic compounds and chlorophyll corpuscles do not persist or come into existence in nature on their own account at the present day, and consequently it is necessary to postulate [guess] that conditions were once such that this did happen although and in spite of the fact that our knowledge of nature does not give us any warrant for making such a supposition.... It is simple dogmatism—asserting that what you want to believe did in fact happen.[5]

Do you begin to see the illogicality of a theory that says the *indescribably complex, ordered, beautifully functioning* world around you and inside you came about by chance?! Do you begin to see how illogical it is to have faith in evolution, the illogical, nay, the *impossible* theory?

Special creation—as overwhelming, as incredibly difficult a realization as it may be—is the only logical explanation for the abundance of the incalculably complex "natural" things around us. When we give ourselves the lifelong task of seeking to understand this great plan and why we and you are the highest creations of all in that plan, then we will have begun to apply the facts, be logical, and gain wisdom.

As you know, before most people can genuinely involve themselves in thinking about special creation and *all that must mean,* they must *know* that it is the answer given to us by logic and science. They must *know* that evolution is the false theory. (Many people *feel* it is the wrong theory but do not know it, hence are not convinced.) They must realize that there are only two theories of how the world and all that is around it, in it, and on it got here. They must understand better than they have ever understood anything before that if one theory can logically and scientifically be *proven* to be false, then only the other remains and each person must cope with that fact in his own way.

No amount of evidence, we feel, can be too much if it is designed to expose the wrong theory and get people to thinking about a Creator, why He purposed to create this world, what He expects from us, if anything, how we should show our gratitude. Yet, since the evidence is mountainous and much of it will require excavating by experts in the various scientific fields, we—as mentioned before—are limiting ourselves to presenting a sampling of what is available. In that vein, several other examples—as logically persuasive as we can make them—follow.

Newton's Model

That a maker is required for anything that is made is a lesson Sir Isaac Newton was able to teach forcefully to an atheist-scientist friend of his. Sir Isaac had an accomplished artisan fashion for him a small scale model of our solar system which was to be put in a room in Newton's home when completed. The assignment was finished and installed on a large table. The workman had done a very commendable job, simulating not only the various sizes of the planets and their relative proximities, but also so constructing the model that everything rotated and orbited when a crank was turned. It was an interesting, even fascinating work, as you can imagine, particularly to anyone schooled in the sciences.

Newton's atheist-scientist friend came by for a visit. Seeing the model, he was naturally intrigued, and proceeded to examine it with undisguised admiration for the high quality of the workmanship. "MY! What an exquisite thing this is!" he exclaimed. "Who made it?" Paying little attention to him, Sir Isaac answered, "Nobody."

Stopping his inspection, the visitor turned and said: "Evidently you did not understand my question. I asked who made this."

Newton, enjoying himself immensely no doubt, replied in a still more serious tone. "Nobody. What you see just happened to assume the form it now has."

"You must think I am a fool!" the visitor retorted heatedly, "Of course somebody made it, and he is a genius, and I would like to know who he is."

Newton then spoke to his friend in a polite yet firm way:

> This thing is but a puny imitation of a much grander system whose laws you know, and I am not able to convince you that this mere toy is without a designer and maker; yet you profess to believe that the great original from which the design is taken has come into being without either designer or maker! Now tell me by what sort of

reasoning do you reach such an incongruous conclusion?[6]

By what sort of reasoning indeed!?

Monkeys, Apes, and the Like

A lot has been written about monkeylike and apelike animals. Evolutionists and antievolutionists have both drawn attention to these animals to make their points. So triumphant is the theory of evolution today, however, that the average person is probably unaware of the evolutionist's retreat from some of his chief theories regarding these animals. Moreover, there are examples that can be made from common experience that can do yet further damage to that strange, irrational myth that holds such sway over the minds of men, the true opiate of the masses, evolution.

First, for those of you who haven't heard, evolutionary scientists have largely given up on the idea that man descended from the apes or some similar looking creature. Nor do they say we came from monkeys. The current view is that man, apes, chimpanzees, monkeys, baboons, orangoutangs, etc. all evolved from something that came before the oldest monkey and then branched off into our own kind.

Permit us to cite some proof that this is *the* present scientific view:

> The living anthropoids, in spite of all their differences, share several so-called anthropoid characters.... Yet the theory of evolution demands that man and these anthropoids have descended from a common ancestor.[7]

Collier's Encyclopedia for 1971 relates that:

> ... scientists infer on evolutionary grounds that

the anthropoid apes and man have a common ancestor.[8]

In *Your Heredity and Environment* by Scheinfeld we find:

> ... mankind descended not *from* apes, but *with* them ... from some remote common ancestor.[9]

(Scheinfeld also reminds us of the interesting genetic facts that: 1) all humans are fertile with one another; 2) apes and monkeys and other simians are not fertile with one another.)[10]

Vernon Reynolds, in a chapter of his book called *Evolution of the Apes,* writes about these "Prosimians" (the ones before the monkeys) and how they were "more widespread and numerous than they are today. There are," he notes, " ... three living families, the lemurs, the lorises, and the tarsiers, which are living in much the same way as these earliest forerunners of apes and men. ... "[11]

One of the "best known" of these pre-apes "inhabited both the Old and the New World [and] varied according to species from squirrel size to the size of a domestic cat, and probably looked more like a rodent than a primate."[12]

Then a scant "thirty millions of years of evolution take us to the middle of the Eocene period (45 million years ago), where we find these animals had progressed," in that they had "an enlargement of the forebrain (and) stereoscopic vision."[13] Reynolds then notes a bit of a puzzle about the Eocene finds, but solves it by sheer evolutionary faith:

> However, interesting though these fossils are, all the ... finds so far are of fossil prosimians belonging to genera that have either died out or have

> close affinities with the lines leading to present-day lemurs and tarsiers. There must have existed, at the same period, a prosimian stock that was capable of evolving into the Old World monkeys and apes. The only fossils that could possibly fit into this category are a few jaw and tooth fragments from Burma ... which may in fact lie on the line of evolution from prosimian to Old World monkey....[14]

One more stage may be noted. Abracadabra!:

> Thus, although the evidence from the Oligocene comes only from one site, and is based on only a few fragments of bone, teeth, and skulls, there is enough to show that already, over 30 million years ago, the higher primates had differentiated into a number of forms that later gave rise to monkeys, apes, and man himself.[15]

Few facts can be noted among these postulations, so let's rerun the main postulations:

1. Prosimians (pre-monkeys) smaller than cats and looking like rodents and very similar to present-day lemurs, lorises, and tarsiers, are the earliest forerunners to apes and men.

Comment: Not one iota of evidence exists for this Brobdingnagian guess! No intermediate, "evolving" fossils have ever been found. No observations of anything but lemurs being born from lemurs have ever been made. The mathematical probability of mutations (which hip scientists such as Mayr discount anyway, remember) producing man or even an ape from these big rats in merely 45 or 30 million years is *absolutely zero!* And the dating methods used to establish the length of time are anything but proven as you have seen. Still, most "scientists" accept Reynolds's account as the way evolution happened....

2. "There must have existed, at the same period, a prosimian stock that was capable of evolving into the Old World monkeys and apes." "There must have existed..."! How scientific is that?!
3. Some jaw and tooth fragments from Burma may be the ancestors of the Old World (European) monkey. Proof? None whatever.
4. Though there are only a few bone and teeth fragments from one site, this "evidence" is enough to declare that the higher primates had split up into different forms from which monkeys, apes, and Albert Einstein arose. Very, very scientific!

But let's leave Reynolds, whose monkeyshines are no more or less curious than any other evolutionist's tales, and let us now open at random another expensive volume on primates from the public library. Here we are on pages 96 and 97 of *A Lesson in Animal Behavior:* "Reactions of Spider Monkeys to Man." The author is a psychologist—one of many over the years who have gotten grants to study the behavior of various animals so that they may learn more about human behavior. That is natural enough if we evolved from them, but since even scientists don't claim that nowadays, it all seems a bit wasted—unless, of course, some humans with behavioral problems were actually cured from what was learned by working with monkeys in spite of the current view that we didn't evolve from them.

The specimen we have randomly turned to was written in the early 30s in Panama. With the right timing by a good comedian, we think it would score very well on TV or radio or stage. But only part of our purpose is to laugh evolution to death; a more important one is to expose the unscientific extrapolations that are the stock in trade of evolutionists. This short piece has its share. We note here only three.

Describing their reactions when approached, he notes that they ... begin barking ... frequently approach the observers ... may growl ... shake the branches ... with either the hands or feet ... while the animal hangs by its tail ... vigorous scratching occurs.... There may occur along with these actions, running movements of the hind legs while the animal hangs suspended.... *These may possibly be incipient escape movements*[16] (emphasis ours).

If the animal made certain movements, then tried to escape, we would know that those were escape movements. If he made the movements and did not seek to escape, by what logic or scientifically supportable reasoning can one attribute the movements to escaping? "May possibly be"! "incipient"!

Later on, after the monkey has thrown every "missile" he can get his hands on at the good psychologist, he (the psychologist) reports:

> This behavior cannot be described as throwing, although the animal may cause the object to fall away from the perpendicular by a sharp twist of its body or a swinging circular movement of its powerful tail.[17]

He can't describe the behavior as throwing, then he describes how the monkey throws something. Peculiar. Not only does the monkey throw things at the intruder, he releases "fecal matter and urine with reference to him." Those actions are described as defensive objectives. Strange language, stranger interpretations.

The summary indicates the monkey's reactions when man approaches. First, he acts aggressive, a bluff, it turns out. Then "flight reactions are shown" which our panel interprets as "he runs." The group then "splits up into a number of subdivisions." They run off in bunches??

But the third and final point gets the prize.

> Animals that have been hunted and shot at remain perfectly quiet and partially concealed when they are approached. This type of defense reaction is very effective in causing one to overlook the animals.[18]

Bear with us while we try to figure this out. . . . If someone shot at a monkey and didn't hit him, would the monkey know he had been shot at? Doubtful, but maybe so. If a monkey had been hunted but not caught, would he know he had been hunted? Extremely doubtful, but let's say Yes. Would a monkey who had successfully avoided being shot or caught by running as fast as he could change his tactics to hiding quietly and partially concealed till a hunter with a gun passed by? Well, it's not impossible, you must admit. But, now we come to the impossible. If this extraordinary monkey figured out all this strategy and hid so well that he caused the hunter to overlook him, how did the hunter know he was lurking there partially concealed??

And, so, another advance in Comparative Psychobiology. . . .

Monkeys, etc.

The Harvey Abstract Saga: There is a fairly common intellectual abstraction that involves monkeys, typewriters, Shakespeare, and infinity. The lesson the abstraction is supposed to teach is that, given enough time the impossible becomes possible. Since this is the exact position taken by evolutionists, it is worthwhile to examine this abstraction, even though it is supposed to be beyond solving by its very nature.

The abstraction itself can be stated quite simply, and is usually put as a question: "If there were an infinite number of monkeys seated at an infinite number of typewriters with an infinite supply of paper for an infinite period of time, could one of them (or all of them for that matter) produce by random striking of the typewriters the works of Shakespeare?"

The answer is supposed to be Yes. If you don't agree, you will be told that you don't understand what infinity is. This shouldn't make you feel bad because infinity is only "one of the most recalcitrant problems of natural philosophy.... [It] has troubled thinkers since the days of Zeno...."[19] So, you quibble a bit and get nowhere. Since, however, this type of unprovable smoke screen is the same type as the one thrown up by evolutionists to explain why something that could not happen happened, let us try to see where it really leads.

First, let us get rid of the typewriter-Shakespeare example and substitute something else. No one can refuse us this. We are keeping an infinite number of monkeys and an infinite period of time and those are the main criteria. If infinity can make the impossible possible, there is no reason why one must stick to one dumb example. Right? Or, not right?

Very well, let's change just one thing in the abstraction. Give the monkeys an infinite number of pencils and pencil sharpeners (this is not unfair ... they had to change ribbons before ...). Let them now produce Shakespeare's works—in English preferably—with proper capitalization and punctuation, naturally.

"It's harder," would be the reply, "but given infinity they could do it," replies Harvey Abstract, our guest abstractologist.

Foiled again, right?

Let's try again. This time let's have an infinite number of monkeys leave their typewriters and pencils behind and attack some simple problem such as growing wheat, harvesting it, and making bread. (The necessary tools are all there just as the typewriters and pencils, etc., were all mysteriously there.)

There they go! Can they do it?! They're working on it! A hundred million years... two billion years... eleven trillion times four quadrillion years. "How are they doing?"

"They did it," you say, Harvey?

"Well, maybe.... But we sort of had the feeling they would be at the same stage at any point in infinity that they were the first day they started. But, Harvey, you've got a powerful argument. Infinity. Wow!"

The plausibility of Harvey Abstract's argument is really impressive, you will have to admit, and we are probably going to have to give up eventually because the argument is so reasonable, rational, logical, and scientific, that it doubtless is beyond challenge.

Just the same, let's have another go at it.

Harvey is now quite willing to agree that some endeavors would take a while longer to bring about by chance, but he still says they could happen, given infinity. There is only one thing to do with an argument that is nonsensical, we have found, and that is to elaborate upon that absurdity until it proves something.... (That sounds pretty abstract too, but it's possible.) Let us take the monkey-infinity thing to yet another level of difficulty, to illustrate.

We want these monkeys—unlimited by number or time—to take from the resources of the earth (as man has) the different metals, plastics, fibers, ink, etc. that make up a typewriter, process them, design the machine, manufacture it and the paper, make up a language that embodies the multitudinous moods that Shakespeare evokes and then reproduce his works. While they are doing that, let them also be taking from nature (where everything is coincidentally located just for the right intelligence!) the graphite, wood, paint, metal, and rubber that goes into a simple pencil. Let them do some more things that man does. Let them write music and make instruments that will play it, and train the other monkeys to make it live from the written sheet, then send it out over TV in color or over AM—FM. (Snap on your portable radio. Amazing, isn't it? Man found out how to use radio waves; he did not and could not create the atmospheric conditions that make them possible!) Let these monkeys design all the marvels man has evolved over the centuries (there's your *only* evolution). Let them think the thoughts and express them in art works, sports, religion, politics, manufacturing, war, and everything else.

We know that Harvey Abstract is going to be unimpressed.

"Naturally it will take longer to do these things," he will say. "Zillions of eons, maybe, but, logically, if they could type Shakespeare, they could do anything, given infinity," he would say.

"Okay, Harvey, you win. But now we want to ask you for your most truthful, most objective, most simple answer—yes or no—to this abstraction.

"At the *very* earliest, according to evolutionists, monkeylike animals appeared on the earth no more recently than fifty million years ago. They were not the most highly developed. There was not an infinite number of them, obviously; in fact, they were *quite limited in number*. They did not have an infinite amount of time, they had barely fifty million years. Could they,

Harvey—now think about it—could this limited number of monkeys in the relatively short span of time have developed even the graphite pencil?"

Harvey is abstract, but he's not crazy.

He says No, without hesitation.

Then Harvey was asked to listen to a few things and to see if he disagreed with any of them:

1. The period of time that animals and man have had on earth is *finite;* it is not infinite. (Monkeys have been around less than fifty million years, and man has been around one million years according to evolutionists. Those are finite periods of time). 2. Monkey-types, evolutionists say, either turned into man or man started out on his own branch of development looking something like a present-day tarsier. Others "would derive man from a fully fledged brachiator;... others ... would prefer that [man's] ancestors were semi-brachiators (arm swingers)."[20]

"In other words, Harvey, evolutionists who base the whole complex world around us on *one totally unproven assumption or another* would say that in a finite number of years some kind of monkeylike animal was to turn into man. 3. Not only is the length of time finite, Harvey, the number of animals that man is supposed to have come from is also finite. 4. Now, Harvey, give us your objective answer. If the animals that were supposed to have evolved into man were on this earth in limited numbers, what would be the chances, in your estimation, of them developing a jet plane or a grand piano in fifty million years?"

Harvey, an altogether able person when he quit leaning on meaningless abstractions, responded quickly.

"Nil," he said. "A limited number of whatchamacallems, in 50 million years would not even produce a wheel," he added with a tone of complete certainty.

"Okay, Harvey. Now if there is *no* chance that the whatchamacallems could have developed a jetliner and all the rest, yet we have these things, man alone was capable and responsible, right?"

"No doubt about it."

"The brain of man is many, many times more capable when it comes to building jetliners and all the rest than the brain of the whatchamacallems?"

"Indubitably."

"Now, Harve, all evolutionists agree that evolution is a purposeless, mindless, random, physical thing. A monkey could not *want* to enlarge his brain so that he could make things of which he has no concept (typewriters, jets, and all the rest), could he?"

"No way."

"In other words, these monkeys could not *plan* to increase their brain size and change physically because they don't know how to *want* things that aren't beneficial to them in their monkey world. Is that right?"

"Quite."

"So all the changes in physique and all the incredible differences in mind that separate man from this ratlike early monkey would have had to evolve by random mutations and natural selection?"

"It would seem so."

"And there would be only a limited number of monkeys and a limited amount of time?"

"Yes."

"Now, Harvey, give us a straight answer; how many whatchamacallems and how long a period of time would be required for them to change physically and mentally into human beings, do you think?"

"Oh, an infinite number for an infinite period." Harvey said confidently, thereby torpedoing a century of evolutionists' abstractions.

"Do you mean that it couldn't have happened in a limited time with a limited number?"

"Impossible, just impossible."

"But, Harvey, that means that man didn't evolve!"

"I know! I know!"

Epilogue: Thus did Harvey Abstract change from always looking at important matters through the distorted prism of evolutionary thought.

"The more I look into the whole business," he told us weeks later, "the more balance I can see in nature, the more purpose I can see in my own life. Evolution is so *stupid* when you think about it!" (Harvey *was* becoming a different person!)

"Why would the whatchamacallems change into something else anyway?" he asked animatedly. "They must have been well adapted the way they were or they wouldn't have survived. Even the evolutionists tell us that." (Harvey had been doing some homework of his own.) "And what would make them change so painfully slowly toward something that would take them out of their trees for which they were well-equipped to survive? They couldn't *know* they were moving toward becoming beer brewers and submarine commanders! And to say that they became these things by mutated accidents has got to be a mad abstraction!" (Harvey, still gesticulating about the silliness of it all, bade us good-by, jumped on a passing bus, sat down, took a banana from his lunch, peeled it halfway, took a bite while scratching the top of his head with his other hand, and, looking at us as the bus pulled out, uttered several rapid chimpanzeelike sounds, "oo,oo,oo,oo,oo," to the obvious amusement of the other passengers.

"Doesn't Harvey seem much happier these days?" I said offhandedly.

"Oh, infinitely!" came the reply.

Superlemur

It is necessary to mention again a couple of points noted earlier in order to bring out a further logical inference against evolution. One of these points concerns the dominant view among evolutionists, the view exemplified in Scheinfeld's statement that "... mankind descended not *from* apes, but *with* them ... from some remote common ancestor."[21] And the other point, also made by Scheinfeld, is that:

> Wherever tested, people of all races and subgroups have proved fertile with one another. This is not true for apes and monkeys—which include many varied species differing in their genes and chromosomes (some radically so) and all of which are infertile with one another....[22]

The older view that man evolved directly from some ape type or other was doubtless too easy an argument to attack, for, after all, there were plenty of ape types around and nobody saw any of them giving birth to anything but their own kind. But pushing the whole question back to a "common ancestor" does not help the argument either. The lemur, the tarsier, and the lorises—all of which are supposed to represent animals very much like the "common ancestor"—are all around too, and none of them have been observed giving birth to anything but their own kind. The whole point of "common ancestor" is logically driven back (logically in evolutionary terms only!) to the "common ancestor" of every living animal on earth, some one-celled microscopic animal in the sea. But these one-celled forms of life are all around today too, they haven't changed into anything else, nor has anyone ever observed an individual among them producing an offspring any different from the parent. Yet, as was seen under "kinds," evolution demands what nature doesn't and can't do. As they are all aware, and as Dobzhansky summarizes:

> All living things grow and reproduce their like.... This process of self production, of like begetting like, is the essence of heredity. Heredity is ... the antithesis of evolution.... Evolution is a process which makes the descendants unlike their ancestors.[23]

So, with all that said, let's look again at the "common ancestor" that is supposed to have given birth to some eleven families of primates, including apes, gorillas, baboons, gibbons, chimpanzees, orangoutangs, marmosets, many different species of monkeys, and assorted other simian types, not to mention man. Some of these are smart, some dumb. Some have long tails, some short; some have no tails. Their teeth vary in number. Some have thumbs, some don't. Their genes are different. Their chromosomes don't jibe. Their blood isn't the same. Only monkeys can breed with monkeys, apes with apes, chimpanzees with chimpanzees—just as man can breed only with his own kind. The nonhuman primates have, in short, an enormous number of differences among themselves, but more important, they have impossible differences from man. The fact that they have fingernails and that some of the smarter ones can be trained to put pipes in their mouths or ride a scooter or some such, and walk more or less upright is very little similarity indeed when compared to the differences.

So what a miracle this "common ancestor" must have been! *Superlemur*—that would have to be its name! Able to leap genetic codes in a single bound! Able to produce offspring that will turn into anything from a marmoset to a man! Able to produce by accident what scientists cannot even define in the lab! So strong and adaptable that he disappeared without a trace! Oh, mighty Superlemur, you are the bright hope of the evolutionists' cult! Return again that all may see and believe your miracles! Return, *Superlemur,* Return!

Thumbs

There is one species of monkey, the spider monkey, that has no thumbs. The spider monkey is not the earliest "evolved" monkey, evolutionists would agree. He is as big as a house cat, fairly trainable, and, in general, is an interesting specimen of the primate order of mammals that includes man and the apes, monkeys, marmosets, and lemurs.

Curiously, animals in the same family as he, which evolutionists say evolved before him, had thumbs. Just as curiously, animals in the same family which supposedly evolved after him also had thumbs.

Of course, the seeming problem to evolutionists can be explained away by saying that the spider monkey just developed out of the main stream, a clan of mutants where the mutation is benign. Or some such.

The difficulty with this sort of monkey business is that all we find in the evolutionists' gallery of living things (from which we sprang somewhere along the line) are exceptions. Everything seems fully developed and functioning properly with all the world's animals, and when they have no thumbs their offspring have no thumbs. Yet the more scientists retreat behind some new blurry excuse, the more followers they seem to have. Hardly anybody is watching the evolutionists! They've got the world convinced, and yet, exposed in plain terms, their theory wouldn't persuade anybody. That's the whole truth of the matter.

Take the spider monkey again. Side track him out of the mainstream of man's evolution. Then, do the same *with all the other living creatures* of the earth, for none among them is one true forebear of man. If some animal were our forebear, that animal would be having offspring different from itself. It would be a "missing link." But no such creature exists. This only means that evolution had to come from some series of creatures, graduated all the way up from something like lemurs, none of which exist today or have left any fossil records of their developing stages. This only places evolution in its proper class, i.e., an animistic religion requiring completely uncritical faith; a religion offering an absurd life and absolute death as rewards for belief. It is a strange religion to have taken hold of men's minds, but man is so enamored and fearful and respectful of anything "scientific" that it has succeeded in spite of being dogmatic and demonstrably unscientific.

A Strange Tail

This will be a short tale.

Some monkeytype animals have tails and some don't. Some of these are put way back on the evolutionary time scale, some not so far back, and some fairly recent. Generally, the little ones have long tails which they use a lot, the thirty pounders have shorter tails which they use some, and the big boys have no tails which they don't use at all.

At first glance, it appears that the tail evolved *off* to prepare man—the ultimate monkey-chimp-ape—for office working and the like, wherein a tail would be a bit of a nuisance. But no one can use the evolution theory to give other explanations even as logical as this for the nature of the monkey tail. What explanation can be given? Are we to believe that as certain beasts noticed they were developing into a larger species, they realized that the day was coming when they would have to make a choice between evolving a really big strong tail or getting rid of the thing altogether?

The first course has obvious drawbacks. Imagine being a three-hundred-pound gorilla of some sort. The tail would obviously have to be six or eight feet long and as thick and strong as a boa constrictor to permit much hanging around. Then, too, many tree limbs would break and that would cause problems. Besides, as already mentioned, later careers such as flint chipping, cave painting, and on through to office working would find them unsuited to their environments.

So a wise decision was made and the word passed down through the generations: "Get rid of the tails; they won't be needed." Animals with tails two or three inches shorter became desirable mates. And with carefully selected breeding the task was achieved on schedule.

The Cow

There is an old joke wherein someone asks a person in a conversational tone if he has read about a machine that has been developed which takes ordinary grass in one end, goes through two or three processes, and gives out pure milk at the other end. Seeing the great value of such a machine for mankind but not having heard the story, the second person says he doesn't know about such a machine, then inquires what the new marvel is called.

The answer, of course, is a *cow*. And just as with every single living thing on this earth, the cow is a miracle of efficiency for obvious purpose. Not a marvel; a miracle! Man can make marvelous things; he cannot make miraculous things. You can prove this to yourself even without the aid of statistics.

Think of the quantity of milk for sale in supermarkets in just the United States right now.... (Don't forget the cans.) Several gallons, eh? Then include milk in all the smaller stores, in milk machines, on milk trucks, in schools, etc. Imagine, then, what is in the refrigerators of just this one country. Keep in mind, as well, that this supply would fall behind if it weren't replenished *every* day.

Then put beside this *large lake of milk* a smaller, separate lake of *cream* that is also replenished every day.

Beside these lakes, picture the mountain of multi-colored *ice cream* that Americans consume on a July day.

And then there is the *butter*. What size village could be built on these lakes by the ice cream mountain just out of the blocks of butter that are produced each day?

And the bricks of *creamed cheese?*

How wide and how long a path could be made from the *cottage cheese?*

What would be the number and size of the mounds of the many different kinds of *cheeses* around Mount Ice Cream?

And this is just in the United States. And just for one day.

Picture, then, if you can, the size island that would be needed to represent the *hamburger* that is consumed each day in this one country.

Envision the size of the canyon needed to accommodate the twenty-two other cuts of meat consumed daily. Top round, bottom round, sirloin, ribs, rump, roasts, corned beef, flank, etc., would all be there.

This is by no means the end, as vegetarians and Hindus will appreciate.

How many leather items can you think of? Purses, belts, wallets, clothing, soap, etc. Quite a few, aren't there?

And keep in mind too that whatever is left of the

cow after she makes these contributions is made into commercial fertilizer—although the cow has been doing her best in this area by contributing right along as a sort of ultimate gesture of her intention to please.

And how many tens of thousands of people earn their living by working solely or partly with the products the cow gives us!

And this cornucopia lives on grass which won't support our caloric needs!

There is nothing designed by man which even approaches this one animal in simplicity of operation, efficiency, or any other business criteria that man employs. And it is only one of the more utilitarian living creatures. All are unique.

We think children could spend delightful hours each day just learning about such wonders as the living things about us. And we believe that no one would have to worry about these students doing their homework, or worry about running low on subject matter. There is more than we can begin to understand in a lifetime.

The Eye

Any eye from any animal provides a good example of the total *illogic* of evolutionary theory. The *human eye* is a subject evolutionists would rather skip:

> To suppose that the eye with all its inimitable contrivances for adjusting the focus to different distances, for admitting different amounts of light, and for the correction of spherical and chromatic aberration, could have been formed by natural selection, seems, I freely confess, absurd in the highest degree.[24]

Who said that? A struggling, obscure nineteenth-century British scientist. His name? Charles Darwin!

Start with a completely developed, fully functioning eye (the only kind that has ever been found!) and work backward a couple of *evolutionary* steps and you will see why Darwin was so candid.

He had no choice.

Take away just one of the "evolved" parts of the eye—let's say the retina—and what do you have? An organ that can see? Hardly! Subtract the lens, or the cornea. Then put the retina back. Could the eye see? Never! It must be complete or it won't function.

By what reasoning or logic, then, would an eyeless creature begin a hundred-million-year project of forming an eye which would be of no use to it whatever until the hundred million years were over? Did these microscopic animals *think* they were developing something that would be useful after a period of time of which even humans cannot begin to conceive? And how many more million years for a fish eye to evolve to be useful out of water?

You've got to have incredible *faith* to believe in such an impossibility. Tertullian (A.D. 150-225) once said: "I believe because it is impossible." The evolutionists are very shortly going to be saying the same thing about *their religion*. The chief difference is that man already has the knowledge to prove the evolutionists wrong. When that is done, Tertullian's "impossibility" will become the only logical, rational alternative. Think about it. There is no other explanation for the balance and beauty in and around us. It is one or the other: evolution or God (see Philosophy, pp. 192-203, for proof). And the mind-staggering intricacy of the eye alone attests to a Designer and Creator who knew what He was doing. When we expel the false religion that all but dominates our institutions and our very lives, and open our deadened brains to this astonishing reality, we shall surely find out what He meant for us to find out. Only an illogical, bumbling god would have it otherwise.

Sam: The Quasi Amphibian—A Farce

If there is any disagreement among evolutionists about man (life) originating in the sea, we haven't encountered it. From the sea, then, so goes the legend, very early man (fish) came onto the land for various lengths of time and established himself as an amphibian. From there it was easy to become a reptile, then a bird, then a mammal, then a man. These later developments are so reasonable and easy to understand that we will ignore them here and just speculate about the evolutionary jump from the water to land.

Let's personify the first fish to make this transition. Call him Sam. (This is not flippant. . . . Nobody knows his name or if it was a he or anything else. All we know is what we are told, viz., that life evolved from fish to amphibians, and so on. So this is quite serious. If it is also ludicrous, that is not our fault; many things that people think are serious are ludicrous, and many things people think are ludicrous are serious.)

Sam, unlike other fish who find themselves ashore, did not die. He was probably there only a few seconds and a wave recovered him. Anyway, he must have liked the feeling of being there, for he went back again and again. In and out of the water, strengthening, no doubt, the lungs he was growing, and the left hind foot that was appearing. He continued to go into the water to eat, we can be sure, because there were no insects or anything around, he being the first animal to come out of the water and evolve. In fact, we can't be sure what it was that drove Sam to act in this fashion. What was the strange fascination? A longing for solitude, perhaps, or some primeval manifest destiny?

Anyway, his lungs and foot were coming along and it seemed only right that he should begin to think seriously about raising a family. Being a very advanced fish (or a very retarded amphibian), Sam preferred to mate with someone his equal. But this proved a futile wish because mutations are extremely rare in the first place, and besides they are too slight to be visible when they do occur. So Sam settled finally on a mate, an attractive normal fish who was willing to put up with his strange behavior (Sam going ashore so much and coughing a lot when he was in the water).

They felt that they owed it to themselves and posterity to pass on the wondrous facility Sam had developed for living both in and out of water.

In due course, Sam and his mate had some fish eggs (not amphibian eggs). Several survived, a fact for which they were grateful; but they were very disappointed all the same. They discussed the matter both in and out of the water and they both grew old and died without figuring out what had gone wrong. They had had such plans for their baby fish . . . or amphibians, that is. But the plans never worked out because all of the youngsters were only fish. They didn't even have the left hind foot, much less another one that they had hoped for. Nor could they breathe out of water.

So Sam and his mate fossilized themselves in a *very* secret place (no "developing" fossils have ever been found) without ever having figured out that acquired characteristics cannot be passed on to offspring.

Had they lived another billion or so years and gained the ability to understand scientific reasoning, Sam and his mate would still be perplexed. They would note that scientists such as Lamarck and Darwin* and Lysenko, a century later, fell into great disrepute among their fellow scientists for insisting that acquired characteristics could be inherited. (Sigmund Freud never changed from this view.) Sam would know the other scientists were right in mocking such an idea. Hadn't he and his mate seen with their own eyes (they had evolved eyes already) that neither their offspring nor their grandchildren nor the next dozen generations had any sign of a foot or any evidence of lungs?

It was a stupid idea. Inheritance of acquired characteristics—Hah!

But they would have been even more baffled and amused to learn that the other scientists (the correct ones who pooh-poohed Lamarckianism) held an even

---

*It is a fairly well-kept secret that Darwin came back around to Lamarckism which he had rejected in his earlier days. We will cite three indications of this fact. An old book (1916) notes:

> Lamarck's name is always associated with the application of the theory of inheritance of acquired characters. Darwin fully endorsed this view and made use of it as an explanation in all of his writings about animals.[25]

This judgment remained steady a half-century later (1968) when Prof. Hotton had Darwin admitting about Lamarck:

> The conclusions I am led to are not widely different from his.[26]

But a longer, more satisfying statement *and* explanation can be seen in this 1967 edition of *A Book That Shook the World*, a collection of "Anniversary Essays on Charles Darwin's *Origin of Species*." In it the various evidences for evolution are noted and the fourth category has been summarized. Then Reinhold Niebuhr continues:

> The fifth category of evidences for evolution was discussed very imperfectly and very hesitantly by Darwin himself. These were the evidences derived from a knowledge of heredity. Darwin says very early in *The Origin of Species* that unless differences are hereditary, they have

stranger belief. These scientists maintained that amphibians came from fish! This, too, they knew was wrong because experience had shown them that Edward Blyth really had the right idea about natural selection, not Charles Darwin.* Moreover, they had seen with their own aquatic fishes' eyes that there would be none of the tasty insects around for him and his mate to eat once they lost their gills and became true amphibians. It was all too ridiculous. It upset Sam so that he woke up ... and swam away.

(Authors' note on Sam: Evolutionists may protest that certain aspects of this farce are unnecessarily misleading or inaccurately labeled. They may say that Sam's foot was a mutation rather than an acquired characteristic, for example, and, hence, could be passed on. But,

---

> no significance for his theory. He was, therefore, very deeply interested in the nature of heredity. He spent a great deal of time studying hereditary variations, but arrived at no satisfactory knowledge of how characteristics are inherited. He was not acquainted with the work that Mendel even then had begun in far-off Bohemia. Later, one of his critics, an engineer named Fleming Jenkin, put his finger on this weak spot in Darwin's theory of evolution. Jenkin pointed out that if inheritance was what Darwin himself supposed it to be and what it was generally thought to be at the time, a kind of permanent and perpetual blending of whatever characteristics were present in the parents, then the variations present in any generation would rapidly disappear through the blending process. How then could they serve to become the origin of new species as Darwin supposed? Darwin realized then that in every generation there must be an origin of *new* hereditary variations more than sufficient to replace whatever was lost. Being at a loss for this, he lapsed into a belief in the inheritance of acquired characteristics.[27]

*Blyth, you may recall, was discussed in the section under Natural Selection, pp. 32-41. He maintained that natural selection would only work to keep a species constant, rather than cause it to change in the extraordinary ways that Darwin envisioned (see also Appendix under Edward Blyth, pp. 217-218).

since mutations are invisible [unless this is Goldschmidt's "hopeful monster"] and since they are regressive or lethal—what *is* a positive mutation anyway?—and further, since we have shown that there are famous biologists who deny that mutations can account for evolution, we chose to fall back, as Darwin did, on acquired characteristics.)

Actually, one simply can't discuss the really important specific aspects of evolutionary theory—such as the transition from sea to land, from fish to amphibian—without being overcome by the absolute ludicrousness of the specific developments that would have had to have happened in any such transition. Rather than defend Sam, we suggest that the burden of *logical* proof is on the evolutionists. Let any one of them take a specific example such as Sam and make him into the first fish-amphibian. Let them tell *exactly* how this happened in a *logical* way, because, after all, if it happened, it had to be logical and that means each development had to be describable. Let them not say " ... then after a period of approximately sixty million years ... " such and such happened. This will just be falling back on one of the most specious of all the evolutionists' assumptions, namely, that Sir Charles Lyell's geologic theory of uniformism or uniformitarianism is valid. Darwin thought it was and based his whole theory on Lyell's theory. Darwin was not a geologist, of course, and Lyell was a lawyer. Baron Cuvier, the foremost geologist of Lyell's time, rejected uniformism, as have many able scientists over the years. Uniformism is just another assumption. It is not scientific in fact and cannot be used to prove anything.

So let evolutionists come forward and give logical descriptions of how a protoplasmic mass became fish and fish became amphibians and amphibians became reptiles and reptiles became birds and mammals and mammals became man, or whatever order this super myth proposes! Evolutionists have always hidden under cover of immense periods of geologically undisturbed time; they have hidden behind similarities of structure and form which do not in any way prove origin; and they have hidden most of all, we think, behind the fact that the whole evolutionary process cannot, after all, be done over experimentally to prove it to doubting Thomases. They have simply implied that anyone who is able to get rid of his silly religious notions can see that this is really the way it happened.

But even this seemingly safe harbor for evolutionists is capable of being overrun, and easily! The way? Simply this: Let evolutionists describe in *words* what they say happened but can't be proven by experiment!

They must be able to do this or throw in the towel. There is no alternative. The world is sick and growing sicker because evolutionary theory has tried to replace the universal feeling for God in man's mind with a science-sponsored religious myth based strictly on faith. It is time to fight back. Enough is enough!

So, tell us exactly how it happened, evolutionists. No more stalling. No more coy hiding behind the fact that you can't show us how it happened; just *tell* us!

Personally, we know you are going to come up with some farces more amusing than "Sam: The Quasi Amphibian," and, with the rest of the world, we will be eagerly awaiting your first effort.

The Miraculous and the Cambium Layer

There is a Cambrian layer and there is a cambium layer. As was shown in the chapter on fossils, the absence of Pre-Cambrian layer fossils stands as a powerful commonsense argument against the theory of evolution.

And, as will be shown in the following, the presence of the cambium layer in trees is a powerful commonsense argument for creation. At first, when the coming attack on evolutionary theory starts, it is such facts that will count the most.

But once the flimsy defenses of Fort Evolution are overrun by such stark examples of common sense, man will have time to turn his newly opened eyes to the uncountable subtler examples of the common sense of a Creator. Then he will begin to see what is so obvious on every side, day or night, wet or dry, summer or winter. . . . He will see miracles on top of miracles.

The concept of the miraculous is, of course, one of the major stumbling blocks standing between believers in a supernatural power and nonbelievers in such a power. Miracles violate or deviate from the known laws of nature, or at the very least, they go beyond our knowledge of these laws. Putting aside the question of miracles attributed to individuals in man's records, it is easier at first to just appreciate the fact that the miraculous is all about us. Everything we see that was not made by man, cannot be made by him, and every such thing has deviated from known laws to be what it is. In other words, if it is assumed that the earth and all that is on it just came to be as a result of some "big bang" theory, then each of the millions of phenomena is in violation of natural law. Water is miraculous. Air is miraculous, gravity, a duck-billed platypus, and so on, ad infinitum. *Everything* qualifies as the most basic sort of miracle, whether one believes in God or not. The difference lies in the inclination of one to explain all these miracles as acts of God, and someone else to explain them as products of an accident. That's what it comes down to: accidental miracles, or created miracles.

Here, then, it becomes obvious that the miraculous

all about us and beyond us is more logically explained as the product of the ultimate miracle, God, than it can be explained by meaningless, directionless accident! In still other words, one is driven by common sense and logic to accept the miraculous all about him anyway, so why refuse to accept the Maker of miracles, the Greater Miracle? After the deceptive falsehood of evolution is buried, then what greater heights of unreason could be reached, than for one to say, "I will not believe in anything so miraculous as God. I am far too enlightened for that! I attribute the admitted miracles of life, earth, and universe to an accident, perhaps a 'big bang' several billion years ago. And furthermore, all who think otherwise are simply dogmatic, anti-intellectual, simple-minded people seeking to avoid the reality of death. . . ." Or some such.

In any case, all this is the kind of thinking that was generated by visiting the Cypress Knee Museum at Palmdale on Route 27 near Lake Okeechobee, Florida. In this location, Tom Gaskins has spent forty years peeling and revealing the unusual characteristics of a threatened species of swamp cypress trees. These characteristics and the two-thousand-foot elevated walking tour through a cypress stand are a delight for any lover of nature. But one demonstration Mr. Gaskins gives rang a particular bell for the two of us newly awakened to the illogical and unscientific aspects of the theory of evolution.

Gaskins takes a presoaked cypress "knee"—which can be a few inches high to several feet—and cuts off some of the bark so people can see how he gets his museum pieces. When he cuts and peels back the bark, he scrapes together a little moist pile of something without which there would be virtually *no trees in the world*. Tom Gaskins explains that the substance he is showing you is the cambium layer, the agent that makes all the wood in the world.

Cambium is one tiny example of a miracle. Man, with all his laboratories, cannot duplicate, replicate, or approximate cambium. It resists all applications of known laws. It defies explanation as merely another miraculous "accident." The mysteries of the cambium layer, of auxins, of root growth, and the like fill large books. Plant physiologists have a whole language of their own geared to describing and unraveling the ineffable bafflement of plant growth. As with animal conception and growth, every single aspect of plant growth—from root to stem, from bark to fruits, from soil to leaf—is a miracle. One's faith in the power of an explosion in the universe billions of years ago to produce auxins, cambium, or a strawberry is obviously a faith in the miraculous. So a strong faith is already there. All that needs be done is to get it in line with common sense.

The Pre-Cambrian layer of the earth proves evolution is a lie. The cambium layer in a tree proves that the miraculous was not haphazard or accidental. For, as Joyce Kilmer observed years ago, "Only God can make a tree."

Form and Structure Similarities

Look and think—as you have never looked and thought before—at the bone structure of the human hand. Compare it mentally with pictures you've seen of similar bone structures of other creatures supposedly extending back 200 million years (Proconsul 25 mil., Notharctus 50 mil., Ectoconus 65 mil., Phiacodon 200 mil.).[28] Think of all the skull types that were supposed to have preceded man. Call to mind the other *very impressive* drawings and pictures of morphological (form and structure) similarities that you have seen over the years in magazines and books. Fix, if you can, your mind on one thought that relates to all of this "evidence" for man's evolution. Don't let what the book said or what anybody has told you interfere with your one thought, if you can help it. Try. Then answer this question:

Do these similarities prove evolution?

They do not prove it, you say, but they sure do make it look reasonable!

Yes, but this is an assumption, not a scientific fact? Agreed.

And remember, there is not one bone, not one shred of evidence living or dead that shows any transitional links between one picture you are recalling and its "next higher or next lower stage." All animals ever found or seen are fully developed, very specialized, and give birth to offspring just like themselves (except for minor variations in color, size, etc.)*

That's interesting. But all the books show the seal's flipper, and the bird's wing, and the hand, and . . .

Yes, but they assume that similarity of structure and form mean similarity of *origin,* which is a very different matter. If one has the inclination, one can just as convincingly assume that a Designer created these animals, and that just because He had a good design—with the spine and skull and hands and all—he used it in different ways in different animals to fit them to their purpose. That's just being efficient, after all. Standardization of certain parts, and all that. You wouldn't expect GM to throw out their efficient wheel and trans-

---

*We have been amazed to learn that many people base their main trust in evolution on the well-publicized peppered moth in Britain. The briefest of investigations will show that this insect's color change has nothing to do with organic evolution. It is still the same moth. The same kind. All antievolutionists recognize that these sorts of variations go on in nature. But even with heroic laboratory controlled *artificial efforts,* no kind has been changed into another kind (see "Thirty-six Bristles," pp. 138-143).

mission assemblies every year and start over, would you? They modify and change and improve but they don't discard a good thing.

That's pretty far-fetched; people will never believe anything so unreasonable as God. There's no evidence!

The evidence is all around you, my friend. It is just a matter of how you interpret it.

Maybe, but I have a right to accept the assumption that is more meaningful to me!

You are so right. And so does everyone else *theoretically*. The truth is, as you well know because you are a living example of it, that the evolutionist's assumption about bone similarities and *every other assumption they make* is presented to the modern world as proven scientific fact. The result? The right to choose assumptions that you just demanded rather testily, is virtually denied to children and adults of our time, and has been denied effectively to them for two or more generations.

Okay. Since I'm the straw man, what do you want me to say?

Two things. One is that all structural similarities that evolutionists present as scientific proof of man's evolution are based on assumption and are backed by no evidence whatsoever. As, for example, Bentley Glass reports in his book, *Darwin, Marx, and Wagner:*

> There exists a unity of structural plan in various species, a unity which was taken to be an indication of their nearness of relationship. This idea of unity of plan was a very old one. It was the basis of the conception of the "Great Chain of Being," about which Arthur O. Lovejoy has written so fully. It does not necessarily involve the idea of evolution at all. Similarities of body plan may exist among different animals without their having

evolved from one another. The same is true of plants. In fact, one of the greatest British biologists, a contemporary of Darwin, Richard Owen, first gave this particular likeness a name, homology.[29]

Okay. All structural similarities that evolutionists present as scientific proof of man's evolution are just assumptions backed by no evidence whatsoever. What's the other thing?

It is this: to be fair to ourselves and true to the scientific method, the case for the antievolutionists must be given equal time in all books, magazines, university fellowships, radio, TV, all schools, and whatever else there is.

Consider it said.

And, let us add a third thing for you to remember. There is nothing wrong with using straw men in debates. Evolutionists have been doing it for years. "Look at the churches," they will say. "See how corrupt and rich and ungodly they are. Who could believe they have the correct assumption." That's one straw man *they* use.

Another straw man evolutionists like to attack is the nonscientist who attacks them. On a TV show about the Darwinian Centennial in Chicago in 1959, Adlai Stevenson, who, of course, was twice a presidential nominee and a widely admired person, responded to one of Sir Julian Huxley's comments with: "I must say that there is a fairly disturbing note in there about the man with no scientific acquaintance who plunges into scientific questions!"[30] Sir Charles Darwin, grandson and namesake of *the* Charles Darwin, and other distinguished guests raised no objection. Irv Kupcinet, the program coordinator from the *Chicago–Sun Times,* caused not a ruffle when he followed Stevenson's comment with: "Some years ago, as a working newspaperman, Governor Stevenson wrote editorials about the Scopes Trial."[31] Get it? Stevenson, formerly a newspaperman, and a highly successful politician the rest of his life, was showing distaste for the idea of nonscientists daring to challenge someone in the sacred fraternity while he—a nonscientist by training or avocation—supported evolution publicly, especially the work of certain scientists much like those with him on the panel. It is a peculiar double standard. If one is not a scientist and says things which support evolution (The Golden Thread of Biology),[32] then he is altogether a brilliant and welcome fellow. If one is a nonscientist and attacks some cherished notion like evolution, then he is altogether an unfit interloper and is disdained by word and deed.

But on the subject of evolution the jury is not going to be made up of evolutionary biologists and paleontologists and other scientists. The jury is going to be made up of just plain people who are going to demand some plain talk. And when they find out just how they have been hoodwinked about the supposed scientific evidence for evolution, they are going to get just plain mad!

Who is to say, after all, that ordinary citizens don't have the right to question *any* group of experts if that group's actions affect the entire spectrum of everybody's life, young, old, working or at leisure? If an engineer designs a bridge and it falls down during the five o'clock rush and kills eighty-two nonengineers, who will say the victims' survivors can make no effective complaint because they are not engineers? If atomic scientists make some little slip and wipe out Oregon, are citizens from neighboring states to allow new atomic sites to be built near them because they feel unqualified as nonscientists in making such a decision?

Too many scientists have enveloped themselves in a

rarefied cloud of intellectual gases and have isolated themselves from the people. In order to get into their club and breathe the heady fumes, one must, of course, have the proper credentials. And you can be quite sure that for one to get the proper credentials he must have the correct view of certain important things, no matter what doubts may assail him from time to time.*

It is a very elitist religious order and heretics are neither welcome nor tolerated. But like all *religious dogmatists* their sanctuary is subject to quick shattering by a world that aches for a philosophy that will fit the order of things and lend purpose and meaning to life. There will have to be a scape-goat upon which the anger of a misled century can be vented. Scientific reputations—those identified with evolution—will have a great fall, and all the king's horses and all the king's men will not be able to restore them again.

Now, permit us to expand the point about similarities of form and structure not adding any proof to evolutionary theory.

It is necessary that you understand three of the key words that evolutionists use to make the point they have made so well and so misleadingly over the years. The first word, *morphology,* you saw a few pages back. It means "the branch of biology dealing with the form and structure of animals and plants." Evolutionists use expressions such as "morphological evidence" quite frequently and they use them as if the words somehow proved their case and as if no further explanation were needed.

---

*Dr. William Tinkle, geneticist, has told us that "some students with good grades have been denied advanced degrees simply because they do not believe evolution." Dr. Thomas Barnes, physicist, has also confirmed that creationist scientists are discriminated against in various ways.

Another word that is used in the same way is "analogy." *Analogy* means "correspondence in function between organs or parts of different structure and origin." Note that *function* is similar. It agrees; it corresponds.

Homology is the third word. *Homology* means (and notice this evolutionary *assumption* in the dictionary!) "Fundamental similarity of structure, regardless of function, due to descent from a common ancestral form; as, the wing of a bird and the forelimb of a horse exhibit homology."

To stick to Webster's example, we can see that a bird's wing and a horse's front leg are homologous because they are similar in *structure* (regardless of function). One could also say they were similar in *function* (regardless of structure), as they both provide locomotion.

One's brain is not strained to see that both these words are appropriate and reasonable, and that indeed there is a morphological similarity between a bird's wing and a horse's front leg. They are both analogous and homologous.

But notice under the definition of analogy that it says "of different . . . origin." One can show similarities of function and structure all day long and not even approach the question of origin. Contrary to the impression that evolutionists give, analogous and homologous functions and structures by themselves *prove nothing* about origins.

Yet the question of origin is what it's all about, isn't it?

Earth—Viewed from the North Star

A reality that should give evolutionists a great deal more pause than it does will occupy us here for a few pages. The reality to which we refer is an order so vast, so complex, and yet so precise in its movements as to defy explanation by the somewhat limited intelligence of man. The reality of a universe completed and in good working order even before Darwin would have us starting out in the primordial sea is, it seems to us, a fact deserving more attention than it gets from evolutionists—or antievolutionists, for that matter. We realize that the evolutionist's subject matter stops as life begins—if one goes from the present backwards in time. Nevertheless, the awesome mystery of the balance and order of the universe should give evolutionists pause in their deliberations and conjectures. It is one thing to defiantly stand on a hill and shake one's fist at an inscrutable cosmos in which the earth may be Wolfe's "unbright and weary cinder" and we may be infinitesimal specks, but it is another to consciously pile up scientifically unsupportable postulations and pipe dreams and press them on a world of human beings who may be *a* or *the* focal point(s) of all this incredible design! That so many people can have the thought at all and even devote much of their lives to the thought of God is proof that minds can be comfortable with this thought. And a comfortable mind, so to speak, is a very close friend of a peaceful soul, so to speak. The same is not true of evolutionary thought because it is *learned,* apparently, far more so than is some feeling for God. No primitive tribes, for example, have been found that had concepts of evolution, but all that have been found have had concepts of God. It may be instinctual. . . . An indefinable intelligence that would design *everything*—even the things we don't understand—would be unlikely to overlook giving us an instinct for feeling and knowing Him! We can suppress it; many do, and that's their business. We were among them; so we understand how *strange* it is to hear somebody actually talking about God as if He really existed. Because of this—and this is a point we emphasize at every opportunity—there is a very serious question to be raised about whether the flabby notions of evolutionists have the *right* to stand unchallenged in schools and in other cultural-transmission and truth-seeking facilities. We would like to see it brought to a Supreme Court test.

In any case, the fact that the wondrous world and universe were there before any life appeared, commands some attention, we think. Indeed, this fact bears obliquely but surely on any critique of evolutionary theory. This is true even if one chooses the "big bang" theory or some other "scientific" nonanswer as to how it all got there ... and here. Toward the end, then, of merely reminding those who haven't thought recently about the intricate movements and delicate balance of all that we see when we look up at night, a few facts about the earth in orbit may be in order.

One believe-it-or-not sort of fact is that the earth's magnetic pole remains pointed almost directly at the North Star all the time during our yearly journey around the sun. Our North Pole (which isn't stationary) misses being in a straight line to Polaris (the North Star) by only one degree nine minutes and in two hundred years it will only be off by two tenths of a degree. A little over four thousand years ago, Alpha Draconis was the star most in line with our magnetic pole, and in a mere twelve thousand years, Vega will hold that position. So, for much, much longer than any of us need to know, the Polestar will serve as a navigational aid, and a pointer to the rest of the stars visible in the Northern Hemisphere.

Though massive and seven times hotter than the sun, the Polestar moves continuously (as does every known thing in the universe) at a blinding speed and yet goes precisely on its appointed rounds, a delicately balanced point of light in a great void that would be far blacker and less beautiful if it and the other stars were taken away. Author Ritchie Calder describes these points of light and their mysterious motions in an interesting way.

> The Milky Way, one such galaxy, consists of 100,000,000,000 "suns"; and two such galaxies are in collision, not head-on, but mingling and interweaving, like the chorus in a Hollywood musical spectacle.[33]

Viewed from the North Star, the earth's eliptical orbit of some 600,000,000 miles would appear very small on a very large chart. The 680 light years (3,988,673,280,000,000 miles) that separate Polaris from us would make the earth microscopic on the same chart, and all of us invisible.

But these facts need not make any of us feel small and unimportant; we are just as big as we were before we read the facts. Besides, there is a galaxy of orbiting "worlds" (atoms) between your upper lip and your nose—if you want to think about something really small, yet still fantastically complex. Or, think of just one of the ten billion cells in your brain; they are pretty small but hardly insignificant, for as you recall, each one is more complex than anything man has built. We are infinitesimally small to the point of being invisible in the vastness of the universe; that much seems beyond questioning. But we *know* this and *think* it. There is *no evidence* whatsoever to indicate that anything else in the immeasurable cosmos has that sort of intelligence no matter how small or large. Except the Creator.

This kind of statement requires a moment's attention to the widely held "theory" that beings similar to us here on earth inhabit innumerable other solar systems in other galaxies. One of us was very fond of this thought and recommended renowned astronomer Fred Hoyle's book, which holds this view, to students for ten years or so. Hoyle brings up the matter four or five times, but this example makes both his and our points best. He asks his readers:

> Will living creatures arise on every planet where favorable physical conditions occur? No certain answer can be given, but those best qualified to judge the matter, the biologists, seem to think that life would in fact arise wherever conditions were able to support it. Accepting this, we can proceed with greater assurance. The extremely powerful process of natural selection would come into operation and would shape the evolution of life on each of these distant planets.[34]

(It is interesting to note this perfect example of professional respect that was mentioned in Part One as reason number five as to why many people believe in evolution. His mention of "the extremely powerful forces of natural selection" indicates a professional trust that can hardly be justified, for as you recall from the Part Two topic of "Natural Selection," it is today anything but an "extremely powerful force" in the eyes of some top scientists.)

Professor Hoyle asks his readers another interesting question, and quotes a biologist in his reply:

> Would creatures arise having some sort of similarity to those on earth? The distinguished biologist, C. D. Darlington, suggests that this is by no means unlikely. To quote Darlington's own words, "There are such very great advantages in walking on two legs, in carrying one's brain in one's head, in having two eyes on the same eminence at a

height of five or six feet, that we might as well take quite seriously the possibility of a pseudo-man and a pseudo-woman with some physical resemblance to ourselves...."[35]

The reasoning behind the conclusion—that manlike beings inhabit other planets in other galaxies—is a powerfully persuasive one, but *only if* one takes evolution to be a fact. If evolution is scientifically and logically proven to be an *impossible concept* under earth's laws, it would then follow that Professor Hoyle and Professor Darlington would be adding just one more unsupportable extension to an already long list of extrapolations about evolution. They would be carrying out just another example of what one might call "Darwin's disease."

One beauty of Hoyle's position is that it seems such a safe theory. As he admits, it is unprovable because intelligible codes that have already been transmitted would require many thousands of years for their answer to reach us. That's a pretty safe theory! It seems to be anyway!

(An interesting aside on this concerns how eagerly such unproven and unprovable "scientific" notions can be welcomed, while mountainous evidence that greets us day and night strongly suggests a Designer and Creator, and this is waved aside as theological nonsense. What motivates this seeming compulsion to pooh-pooh God is an open question, perhaps calling for some psychological interpretation such as megalomania. But whatever motivates, it is not scientific evidence; that much is certain.)

Anyway, as explained, the life-in-outer-space theory is in a symbiotic relationship with evolution. When the host dies, so will the parasite.

But let us get back to our reporting on a few things that would be quite *impossible* to have happened by accident, things that were working well even before there was any life to be explained by any theory.

Some further information about the earth's orbit will serve as well as any example, for, perhaps, it is tailor-made for us. It's all quite a precise business too, of course, and although we don't pay much attention or are not aware, an extraordinary number of things are going on all the time. If any of these factors—none of which man had anything to do with or basically understands—changed in any marked degree, it would be all over for life on earth. For example, we are moving around our orbit at a fantastic speed, and any deviation in speed or course would be disastrous. It's tempting to think of an orbit as a track, but the temptation should be resisted because while the timetable, speed, and distance are all the same, we never pass through any previously traveled spot in the universe, nor does anything else. The reason? All things—sun, planets, moon, meteors, lunar modules—are moving away from somewhere at a speed that is, again, fantastic. In other words, everything stays in its place relative to its sun, planet, moon, etc., but nothing is ever in the same place, because all of these bodies are moving away in perfect synchronization.

None of the incredible speed at which we are moving is evident to us, a rather extraordinary fact in itself, you will agree. Nor are we aware of the turning of the earth on its axis which causes our nights and days and which is calculated at about one thousand miles per hour at the equator.

But let us take a paragraph from Professor Hoyle, who knows these phenomena well. He is writing under the subtitle "Birth of the Stars":

> Now I must introduce you to the idea that this immense disk of gas and stars is in motion, that it

is turning round in space like a great wheel. How then do the stars move? The main motion of a star is along a path that is roughly a circle with its center at the center of the Galaxy. The Sun and the planets move together as a group around such an orbit. The speed of this motion is in the neighborhood of 500,000 miles an hour. But in spite of this seemingly tremendous speed it nevertheless takes the Sun and its retinue of planets about 200 million years to make a round trip of the Galaxy. At this stage I should like you to reflect on how many ways you are now moving through space. In England you have a speed of about 700 miles an hour round the Solar axis of the Earth. You are rushing with the Earth at about 70,000 miles an hour along its pathway round the Sun. There are also some slight wobbles due to the gravitational attraction of the Moon and the other planets. On top of all this, you have the huge speed of about 500,000 miles per hour due to your motion around the Galaxy.[36]

Another phenomenon is the earth's axis, in other words, the imaginary line running through the poles. This axis is not perpendicular to the plane of the earth's orbit; if it were there would be no change in seasons. To improve upon this undesirable sameness there is a convenient "tilt" to the earth's axis at 23½ degrees. But there is no appreciable "wobble" as the earth speeds around the life-sustaining sun in its ceaseless 600-million-mile yearly run. Tilted thusly at 23½ degrees, the North Pole at any place in the earth's orbit thus points its inscrutable magnetic finger at the North Star. There is the interesting fact too, that, although the earth is not perfectly round—it bulges at the equator somewhat, and has high mountains and deep seas—it is, for its size, still more perfectly round than the finest ball bearing that man can make. (Put one under a high powered microscope and you will see.)

These few little mysteries of balance, speed, and distance are as but one grain of sand on the world's beaches, one leaf from all her forests, one raindrop in a thunderstorm. The universe that we can see from horizon to horizon—and infinitely more that we can't see—fairly bristles with an order and structure that thus far has defied penetration by man's intelligence. When man does gain some knowledge about the nature of this or that phenomenon, it is just a discovery of an already operative phenomenon. The discoverer may learn from its behavior and duplicate its principles to some degree in the laboratory and thereby "create" a model or a hypothesis or a theory. But at least two important truths will be very obvious even when this much is achieved: 1) Emulation or copying—not creation—is all that is really being done; 2) A great deal of planning, designing, testing, and constructing will go on in the laboratory just to copy something. The result being sought will not accidentally occur by putting all the equipment and calculations in a room and igniting a box of dynamite, a rough approximation of the "big bang theory," modern astronomy's most sophisticated explanation of how *everything* got to be the way it is!

Perhaps a comment made by Emerson when he was a young man comes close to capturing this whole thought in a sentence:

> Idealism . . . beholds the whole circle of persons and things, of actions and events, of country and religion, not as painfully accumulated, atom after atom, act after act, in an aged creeping Past, but as

one vast picture which God paints on the instant eternity for the contemplation of the soul.[37]

Pollination—A Call to Poets

It takes a poet to do justice to the topic of pollination. The pollination process is so finely and intricately conceived, so essential in the awe-inspiring balance of nature, so incapable of having evolved by accident, that it constitutes a thousand silent proofs of God. These silent proofs need to be given tongues by poets.

But what are the gossamer words to describe wind flowers? What dancing rhyme and meter can capture the loving care that God put into wind pollination?

Must a Greek coral dance be recalled to somehow communicate the wondrous workings of bee flowers, or moth flowers?

What imagery, what onomatopoeia can be rallied to the cause of showing God's plan through water flowers, or beetle flowers?

Lives there a poet who can lead a charge of words so forceful that they prove God? Then let him take the miracle of pollination and do it!

Or perhaps a poetess, finding that mundane themes fail to inspire, can infuse the language with a more subtle logic.

In any case, there is a virtual arsenal of factual ammunition about pollination with which to mow down the theory of evolution and prove God.

There are moth pollinators, in addition to the bees; over 100,000 butterfly species! And there are flowers which are pollinated by the lowly fly—flowers so specialized that they are dull colored and give off odors of dung, carrion, fish, and decaying things. How many eons would be required to evolve even one such phenomenon?

And how many eons to produce the flower that traps its agent and shakes the pollen on?

And there are flowers that birds go to, flowers that attract only them. And flowers that wasps pollinate and return to again and again; for these are flowers that take care of a wasp's sexual need. Is that blind evolution, friend; or God, indeed?

Yes, some poet should roll up his sleeves, spit on his hands, and tell us about miracles such as these! And infinite others across the many lands, and throughout the vast seas.

So, poets, come to mankind's aid, please....

Thirty-six Bristles

Flies—to almost anyone but a geneticist—are merely one of nature's pests.* But to geneticists (biologists who deal with heredity and variation among related organisms) they are extremely important; especially the fly *Drosophila*. There are at least a *thousand* species of this fly, and, because it produces a new generation every twelve days, it is the ideal animal for geneticists to use in the study of hereditary characteristics. *Thousands* of

---

*Flies *are* pestiferous. There is no arguing that point. Yet they perform very specialized and very necessary functions. They help carry out pollination functions on certain flowering plants, as you saw in the section on "Pollination." And so fantastically interdependent are nature's millions of aspects that—according to Eiseley—man could not live without flowers. So their role in this area alone is no minor one. Then, of course, flies are busily occupied with helping to dispose of the tens of thousands of tons of animal and human waste that reappears every day. In addition to this one can imagine that there are tons upon tons of animals and fruits that die every day and are partly removed by flies. Some species of the fly, *Drosophila,* are so specialized in their function that they eat only injured and rotting fruit and do not bother uninjured fruit. (Think about *that* for a minute!)

pages have been written about *Drosophila,* and its critical importance to genetics can be seen from this typical remark from a book called *Genetics and Heredity:*

> *Drosophila* is now used in laboratories all over the world, and from certain points of view one can say that the whole of modern genetics and the science of heredity are due to it. . . .[38]

More up-to-date books by different authors still stress heavily the importance of *Drosophila.*

We wish to stress its importance too, because we intend to show that the work of geneticists on this humble animal has given the most concrete proof that mutations—the life breath of evolutionary theory—could never account for evolution.

With that, permit us to give you an overview and the results of thousands of pages and tens of thousands of hours that science has devoted to studying mutations and their effects on the fruit fly, *Drosophila.*

Keep in mind first what has already been mentioned about *Drosophila* producing a new generation every twelve days. This makes it possible for scientists to study several hundred successive generations which would correspond to fifty or a hundred or more *centuries* of human life. Armed with this knowledge, T. H. Morgan and his collaborators, Bridges, Sturtevant, and Muller, obtained a lot of jars, some yeast and bananas, and a few hundred thousand specimens of *Drosophila* and went to work.

The intention was to observe and catalogue information about mutations. One difficulty about mutations, as you have already seen, is that they are very infrequent, and then of the ones that do occur, almost all are harmful and lead to the early death of the mutant or its descendants. Two other characteristics of mutations that make them hard to study are that there is no way of knowing when one is going to occur, and that most that do occur, according to geneticists, are unnoticeable because their effects are hidden or are so slight that they are invisible. (This we think is pure nonsense. If one can't see a mutation or in some way detect it—if it is invisible—then how can anybody say it exists at all!)

In any case, Morgan published in 1915 his *Mechanics of Mendelian Heredity* which laid the foundations for the arrangement of genes in the chromosomes, and he became the leader of what is known as the "Morgan school" which is known for this kind of work in connection with evolutionary theory.

The upshot of all that was that

> among hundreds of thousands of flies, it was possible to detect, over a period of several years, more than 400 mutations.[39]

Though evolution was supposed to be proven by this Herculean effort, it failed miserably and totally, for

> out of the 400 mutations that have been provided by *Drosophila melanogaster,* there is not one that can be called a new species. It does not seem, therefore, that the central problem of evolution can be solved by mutations. . . .[40]

Given the fact that scientists generally agree that evolution without mutations is about as possible as an egg omelet without eggs, this is a very important finding.

But evolutionists do not give up so readily and there is more to report on their efforts with *Drosophila melanogaster.*

Since the problem that Morgan and his helpers had faced was the scarcity of mutations, it was a big breakthrough when a way was discovered to increase the mutation rate tremendously. From *Principles of Genetics,* we learn that

> H. J. Muller demonstrated in 1927 that the mutation rate of *Drosophila melanogaster* could be markedly increased by treating the flies with X-rays. Expression of induced mutations seemed to be the same as those of comparable mutations that occurred spontaneously, but the frequency was increased as much as 150-fold.[41]

Now, at last, it was possible to really go to work on the hapless fruit fly! Whereas, scientists had labored manfully to bring on artificial mutations by extreme variations of heat and cold and light and darkness, all with complete lack of success, they now bombarded the stubborn rascals with X-rays and got their mutations.

Thus stocked with jars of mutant flies, scientists set about to change them into something besides flies, and thereby demonstrate that animals could indeed have changed from amoebas to fish to amphibians to reptiles, to birds, to mammals, and finally to man.

The reader may protest that the average "evolving" lizard or bat out of the past never had the benefit of all this sophisticated effort to help him along, and would therefore have hardly been able to produce all those mutations in the first place. But the reader would only be exhibiting a stubbornness that seems to afflict non-evolutionists. After all, if things didn't evolve, one would only be left with the reality that they were created; and that just can't be! So say the evolutionary scientists.

So they X-rayed the daylights out of ole *Drosophila melanogaster.* They changed the eye colors from pink to white to red and back again. They changed the wings this way and that. They worked on the salivary glands. They increased and decreased the number of bristles.

They strained and sweated for thousands of hours to change *Drosophila* into something else.

What happened? Two things. One, the mutant flies either died over a period of generations, or, *they came back to their original, normal conditions. They could not be changed! Drosophila melanogaster,* frozen, steamed, blinded by light and darkness, and fried with X-rays, remained *Drosophila melanogaster.*

The case of the thirty-six bristles will serve as a specific example.

Among its other equipment, *Drosophila melanogaster* has thirty-six bristles on its body. (Why thirty-six bristles seems to be just the right number for this creature and what they are for are interesting questions which, as far as we know, were never asked and much less answered by these investigators.) Macbeth gives the gist of further extensive work done on the fruit fly by Ernst Mayr in 1948. (We will add italics to emphasize a few points.):

> Two experiments were run, one for decrease in the number of bristles, which averaged 36 in the starting stock. Selection for decrease was able, after thirty generations, to lower this average to 25 bristles, *but then the line became sterile and died out.* A mass low line ... was started with 32 bristles and remained nearly stable for ninety-five generations. *All attempts to derive from this line others with lower bristle numbers failed because the lines died out....* In the high line, progress was at first rapid and steady. In twenty generations the average *rose* from 36 to 56. *At this stage sterility became severe....* Average bristle number fell sharply *and was down to 39 in five generations.*[42]

Amazing, isn't it? The same thing happens to all breeding experiments, of course, no matter what the animal or plant. Darwin got the same results exactly on a smaller scale after he spent years working with pigeons. There is just so much variability in any animal, and when it is pressed beyond that limit by nature or by man it dies or becomes sterile. In either case, obviously, the kinds of change demanded by evolutionary theory are just as effectively stopped.

A day of reckoning is at hand for the theory of evolution. And amongst the most convincing witnesses to testify against the theory will be one of the most humble, yet most triumphant reminders of God's immutable laws, *Drosophila melanogaster* with its thirty-six bristles intact.

Three Minus One Equals Two, Minus One Equals One

There really isn't much more that we need to say about the theory of evolution. It is either a dead duck or we have failed. Just the same, there is a further word to be said about what might be called the Compromise Theory. This theory accepts both God *and* evolution. As a philosophical position, it became popular enough before Darwin died so that "the dignitaries of the Church were eager to pay him [Darwin] the highest honour."[43]

The poet Tennyson grasped the essence of the dilemma caused by Darwin's theory and its conflict with the creation theory. "Strange," he wrote, "that these wonders should draw some men to God and repel others."[44]

Yet, there were many who saw in the Compromise Theory merely an attempt by religionists to keep the creation explanation alive in the face of the new challenge from science. This view was held, for example, by the American philosopher-educator, John Dewey. A staunch evolutionist and atheist, Dewey saw belief in evolution and God at the same time as "design on the installment plan." And as the passing decades have shown, Dewey was not alone in this thought. Pure evolutionists have steadily risen to a dominant place in the intellectual world; antievolutionists have just as steadily fallen to a position of noninfluence; and those who accept the compromise view have largely occupied the ground in-between.

The welcome news for those who hold to the compromise theory is simply this: Unless evolution can account for *all life without assistance* it has *no status* as a theory. If God "directed," "allowed," or "used" evolution as His means to bring about some—or even all—life, then some or all life did not spontaneously generate itself out of nonliving matter and then evolve by *accidental* mutations and natural selection as evolutionary theory demands that it must! If life could not and did not evolve on the strength of evolutionary theory's own rules, then there is no theory.

In other words, if God created life, then the creation theory stands. It does not matter whether He did it all at once, or in stages; it would not have happened without Him, and is, therefore, His creation, pure and simple.

Once the full measure of this truth is realized, each person will begin to know the full meaning of what Milton felt when he wrote: "In Thy presence, joy entire."

Part Four

WHAT IS NEXT?

(Five Examples of Critically Important Areas of Modern Civilization That Have Been Molded to Fit the Theory of Evolution, and How Those Areas Will Be Affected by the Collapse of That Theory)

Science

Following the publication of Darwin's *Origin of Species*—"the book that shook the world"—evolution theory largely crowded out creation theory in scientific circles within a decade or so. Since that time the spread of evolutionary thought has been rapid in other fields as well. Not only the natural sciences but the social sciences, the arts, and the humanities have accepted the evolutionary concept of life's origin as the central fact of life, and have restructured their disciplines to accommodate the accepted theory. Today it is obvious that evolutionary theory is dominant throughout the intellectual world.

While this momentous change took hold in the universities very quickly, it took longer and was less successful among the general population, even in the more developed countries. Amongst these general populations there was a large percentage which wavered between what a growing band of evolutionists assured them was true, and their traditional belief in creation. Some broke loose from tradition and embraced the new theory quickly and totally. Others reached some sort of compromise. Still others refused to change. The generation now under thirty has doubtless made an unqualified switchover in greater numbers than any before it, though there is evidence that many of these young people are now singularly disoriented and unfulfilled. They and others are searching for something, it seems; something more meaningful than evolutionary explanations for life can give. Communist countries, of course, officially reject the creation theory and officially promote the evolution theory.

In underdeveloped countries where the masses are not so easily reached, and where one religion or another has remained influential, evolutionary thought has made fewer inroads.

This, we submit, is a brief but fair overview of the pattern of world change in the last century relevant to the growth of the theory of evolution and the decline of the theory of creation. Once this total situation is grasped, and its importance understood, it can be appreciated that the destruction of the theory of evolution—its destruction once and for all as a viable option—can hardly avoid triggering a revolution in man's thinking—a revolution that offers unbelievable hope to mankind from an unexpected quarter.

Virtually all books by scientists postulate evolution and proceed as if that theory were fact. The exceptions to this that we found appeared under the auspices of the Creation Science Research Center in San Diego, whose scientists are committed to getting the creation theory taught in the schools.* Apart from these and a few other exceptions, scientists normally proceed with their investigations with this thought as their guideline:

> Modern evolutionary theory is the great unifying concept of biology. It represents the major theoretical triumph of the biological sciences—an all embracing theory which attempts to explain the manifold complexities of biological phenomena.[1]

As has been said, however, and as the following chapters seek to demonstrate, the influence of evolutionary thinking has penetrated far into areas other than science, areas that influence the lives of nations and individuals to a degree that is appreciated by few people. Evolutionary scientists are among the few who are aware of this extended influence. Professor Dobzhansky comments on how far the theory has penetrated people's thinking *outside* of science:

> Today, more than a century after Darwin, the idea of evolution is becoming an integral part of man's image of himself. The idea has percolated to much wider circles than biologists or even scientists; understood or misunderstood, it is a part of mass culture.[2]

Occasionally, a voice of doubt will be heard, but it seems to have little or no effect. This observer of the

---

*Two excellent examples that came recently to our attention are: *Why Not Creation?* and *Scientific Studies in Special Creation,* Walter E. Lammerts, ed., (Presbyterian and Reformed Publishing Co., Nutley, NJ, 1970-1971). These books contain selected articles from *The Creation Research Society Quarterly.*

Also, Evan Shute's, *Flaws in the Theory of Evolution* (Craig Press, Nutley, NJ, 1971) commends itself to those who wish a detailed, impeccably scholarly treatment of the subject.

Darwinian Centennial voiced his own grave doubts without apparent impact:

> Can we ... will we discover the missing links in the chain joining all life on Earth, so that the spiritual and moral status of man at least will not be left offside as an inexplicable unicum that has dropped from the skies, so to speak? Does an incomprehensible gap have to be left just at the peak of the *alleged* evolution ... a vacuum which will be not only a living accusation to science but which *may ultimately make people wonder afresh whether this evolutionary theory has not after all been a huge mistake on the part of an overwrought science?*[3] (our emphasis).

That was in 1959. Now, years later, the voices of the opposition are increasing. To quote but one, Dr. Etheridge, a famous fossilologist of the British Museum:

> Nine tenths of the talk of evolutionists is sheer nonsense, not founded on observation and unsupported by facts. This museum is full of proofs of the utter falsity of their views. In all this great museum, there is not a particle of evidence of the transmutation of species.[4]

Thus the first shots have already been fired in a revolution of which few are yet aware.

The public, of course, has every right to demand that the evolutionists defend their views in a convincing way, or admit the inadequacies of their views, for it is the public, after all, which pays most of the bills. Borek acknowledges this important fact:

> The overwhelming portion of scientific activity is financed by our federal government and therefore by the creators of our total wealth, the American

people. Science and its products are as much the property of the American public as is TVA or the Hoover Dam or a submarine propelled by atomic power. . . .[5]

So the public does have rights in the matter (and not only in the United States). Accordingly, arrangements should be made so that evolutionists can meet with antievolutionary scientists in debate until the issue is settled. Perhaps on TV—or better still, perhaps, "in order to . . . establish justice" for the people, as the American Constitution stipulates—a legal case should be pressed upon the evolutionists, with the intent of having them convince judge and jury that their theory has *any* basis in scientific evidence. There can be no doubt of the outcome. When influential evolutionists such as Huxley, Simpson, Dobzhansky, Mayr, and a few others are forced to admit that they can prove *nothing,* and indeed that all the scientific evidence refutes their claims, Darwin's theory will suffer conclusive and worldwide rejection. Sir Julian Huxley is nearly ninety years of age, the others in their seventies. Their mental faculties are considerable, but they will not face as easy challenges as T. H. Huxley (Darwin's Bulldog) faced in 1860, or Clarence Darrow (Scope's Bulldog) faced in 1925. Today, evolutionists will face the testimony of trained scientists[*] from different fields who cannot fail to point out one simple but devastating fact, namely, that evolutionary theorists rest their case on a fantastic array of assumptions, postulations, and speculations which not only have no scientific support, but are actually refuted at every step by unassailable scientific laws.

Properly handled, the defense, in other words, the

---

[*]See the list of such trained scientist on page 31.

evolutionists, could win a token victory just as William Jennings Bryan did in the Scopes Trial when biology teacher Scopes was fined one hundred dollars and costs. The real victory, however, just as in that trial fifty years ago, will belong to the prosecution which might well follow some variation of the six-stage strategy below:

1. Raise doubts about the credibility of evolutionary theory.
2. Intensify these doubts.
3. Translate doubt into loss of confidence.
4. Demonstrate that without confidence there can be no trust.
5. Emphasize that something in which there is no confidence or trust cannot justifiably be promoted or taught as scientific theory.
6. Conclude that evolutionary theory has no claim to the support of science, and is henceforth discredited as an explanation for the *origin* of life.

Who would not have the keenest interest in such debates and/or such a legal confrontation? "Evolution on Trial" would be an appropriate designation and TV time would be well spent in the public interest. Certainly there was intense interest in the 1925 trial which was instigated and financed by the American Civil Liberties Union under the leadership of Roger Baldwin.[6] The issue then was academic freedom. The issue is the same, only the theory seeking equal time is different. The ACLU could do much to allay doubts about its lack of political bias if they championed this case as energetically as they did the other one.

Of course, the impact of such an undercutting of evolutionary theory will be felt further and wider and faster than was true of the impact of the Scopes Trial. This is true for several reasons having to do with improved communications. But the most important reason is that people *want* to hear this news! There was no man-made force at the Scopes Trial and there has been none since that could stop the spread of what seemed to be the truth. There will be no stopping the spread of the *real truth* which is that "Evolution Is Dead—Creation Theory Is Triumphant!"

This truth has the power to cut across international borders and ideologies; across prejudice and intolerance. The communications are too well established, the hunger for this news too great, to be forestalled once the false theory about the origin of life is discredited.

There are extraordinary changes that can be expected as a result of the collapse of evolutionary theory, not the least of which is *the undermining of the ideological base of Marxism*. This change and others that can be expected are examined in the chapters that follow.

Another brief thought about what can be expected as far as science is concerned has to do with eugenics. When one views man as just another animal, it is easy to get excited over the fantastic "achievements" of eugenicists. One writer reports:

> Man could ... deliberately restrict the perpetuation of some genetic traits and encourage those of others. And now that we have at last learned the genetic code... the day will surely come ... when genes can be altered in order to design, at least in part, new human beings. ....[7]

The question as to who decides what "designs" will be used, and on whom, is raised but not answered. There is talk of letting malaria and other "traditional killers" come back to keep the population down. Those who have misgivings about such "scientific advances" are told that

> we have already gone too far toward modifying *biological evolution* to pull back now.[8]

Reacting to this type of assertion, the National Research Council was moved to ask, "Where Is Science Taking Us?" Their findings:

> The surviving portion of the human race will be different from man as we know him now. He will be harder, and the gentler traits that we now admire, as well as the appreciation of and the need for the beauty of nature, will be bred out of him.[9]

The public should at least have the right to express a view on this sort of license, perhaps through the ballot box. This may not prove to be necessary, however, once the evolution theory is debunked, for, as the author of the following paragraph explains, evolution is the guiding star of the scientific approach to man.

> Whether we discuss man as a biological organism, the aims and premises of civilization, or the meaning of moral or aesthetic judgments, we ask "How did they first appear?" and "What has been their evolution?" We hesitate to ask instead "What is their meaning?" or "To what extent are they valid?" because we are such thoroughgoing evolutionists that we find it difficult to conceive of any meaning or validity apart from origin and development.[10]

The excesses of many eugenicists, and the misdirection of so much scientific skill and public monies, couldn't be more neatly explained than Krutch has done in this short quotation.

In an article, "Why the Growing Disenchantment with Science?" Dr. D. S. Winnail states:

> The glamour that once surrounded science and technology has been replaced by growing criticism and antagonism. Many—including scientists—are concerned over the dramatic shift.[11]

What has happened to cause this change, this swing in the pendulum of public opinion? The same article quotes the answer given by Professor Samuel Silver in *Science Journal:*

> There is a feeling, which is growing in the United States and in other Western countries, that the advances made through science and technology have somehow failed their promise; that the hope placed in them by mankind for the attainment of a more satisfying life and of a happier and more tranquil world has suddenly been betrayed. There is in consequence a growing sense of dismay and frustration regarding science and technology....[12]

Notably, this decline in the public's respect for science and technology is counterbalanced by a corresponding increase of respect for, and interest in, mysticism and religion. If this continues—and indications are that it will—then what we are witnessing is the reversal of a five-hundred-year trend in history.

The sciences started gaining real influence around 1500 and grew steadily more influential down the centuries, right through the 1960s. They are now losing that influence. Today we are more concerned with questions such as "Why does man exist?" and "What is life's purpose?"—questions outside the scope of science.

There were, of course, atheists long before Darwin,

for evolutionary theories can be traced back to ancient times.

But the world in 1859 was ready for Darwin's book. *The Origin of Species,* however, summed up and went beyond what had been said before, and it sold remarkably well. Up to then, those who had turned away from organized religion had done so primarily as a reaction against the corruption, intolerance, and often cruelty of the Roman Catholic Church; defects often equaled in the sixteenth through nineteenth centuries by the Protestants. Thus, out of reaction against the rigidity of the church, and fortified by science in their doubts relating to church dogma, many were ripe indeed for "the book that shook the world."

Few, prior to Darwin, had gone so far as to reject God; it was organized religion that had been under attack. This is not the same as the "God Is Dead" movement that began with Nietzsche in the 1880s and has reached its peak in the last few years.

With the advent of Darwin's theory, and its acceptance by ever-growing numbers of people, religion looked steadily more foolish and science more reasonable. Not only did science appear more reasonable, but it appeared also to be more dedicated to truth.

So, in our century, science took over the leading role. Scientists became the new priests of a new faith. Dr. Winnail notes:

> The one event that undoubtedly had the most profound effect on the decline of religious influence and advanced the cause of materialistic explanation in science was the publication of Darwin's theory of organic evolution. The basic tenets of the theory were so diametrically opposed to existing theological ideas about man and the natural world that a showdown was unavoidable.[13]

The Golden Age of Science is now behind us. It gave the world much, including most significantly, perhaps, an awareness of its limitations. When scientists fully understand that their role is to help reveal God's plan rather than to be God, then, and only then, will they be able to recapture some of the respect they will lose when the evolutionary theory collapses.

Education

After the theory of evolution is laid to rest, important changes will be necessary at all levels of the American public school system; not to mention school systems in other countries. These changes will require a monumental overhauling of educational philosophy. In order to make changes and make them correctly, we must know *what* we want to change and *why* we want to change. Accordingly, we must understand something of the dominant philosophy we have now, and how it got to be where and what it is.

American education carries deep in its blood stream the genes of one man's philosophy. John Dewey is that man. Beginning over fifty years ago at a critical period when the United States was maturing and beginning to emerge as world leader, this tireless philosopher-educator became to American education what Freud was to psychoanalysis, what Darwin was to evolution, what Marx was to communism, what Einstein was to physics. Dewey's books have been required reading in teachers' colleges for two generations. He was "the philosopher who influenced American education more than any other living thinker."[14] In short, Dewey's formative influence on the minds of teachers and children for a half century has had a profound effect on the philosophic direction of this country as expressed through its educated citizens.

What kind of a man was he, this man whose thinking—bolstered by others of like mind—has permeated and spread through our culture so deeply? What, in fact, did he believe? From "Source Problems in Education" we find an important part of the answer:

> John Dewey, whose reconstruction of philosophy fundamentally conditioned modern thought, was himself conditioned by Darwin and evolution. Born in the year the *Origin of Species* was published, he became one of the leaders in an intellectual revolt against formalism in thought and traditionalism in method. Instrumentalism, the name Dewey used to describe his philosophy, reflects its Darwinian temper just as his humanistic naturalism reflects the inspiration of science.[15]

So impressed by the theory of evolution was Dewey, that he wrote an essay to commemorate the fiftieth anniversary of the appearance of Darwin's book. In it, he says:

> *The Origin of Species* introduced a mode of thinking that in the end was bound to transform the logic of knowledge and hence the treatment of morals, politics, and religion.[16]

This was an astute observation for 1909, and, in a sense, Dewey's philosopher credentials are validated on this one point alone. Not being a natural scientist, he could not know that what Darwin and his disciples had proclaimed as truth by 1909, would be quietly abandoned in the coming years.

He did anticipate, however, that a struggle would be necessary to "transform the logic of knowledge." The old philosophies that pointed to God through design in nature and stubbornly leaned on special creation as an explanation for man's origin, were still formidable, he realized. But he predicted that change would come in spite of resistance. He saw the revolution coming:

> The influence of Darwin upon philosophy resides in his having conquered the phenomena of life for the principle of transition and thereby freed the new logic for application to mind and morals and life.[17]

What Dewey envisioned as early as 1909 proved correct. Darwin *did* affect our minds, morals, and lives. This gives us some idea of the massive unlearning, the Herculean deconditioning now necessary to change the educational system in America, and many of our attitudes about life in general. We can face this task confidently, however, for we know that Dewey and others had an equally hard task—maybe harder—and they did it!

Dewey wanted a revolution in thought, and he got it. At the centennial of the publication of Darwin's book, seven years after Dewey's death at age ninety-three, one of the commentaries ran:

> Darwin's critics ... might doubt the originality of his theory and deny its truth, but they had to concede that ... it was revolutionary in its effect.[18]

This is a statement with which everyone can now agree. Darwinism has had a *revolutionary* effect. Not just in biology. Not just in politics. Not just in economics. The effect extends into psychology, sociology, the arts, humanities, philosophy, and other disciplines. Indeed, the triumph of evolutionary thought has been revolutionary in the fullest meaning of that word.

The success of this total revolution was aided immeasurably by John Dewey. He made it stick in the place where all revolutions are guaranteed longer life, that is, in the schools. This method of implanting and reinforcing ideas until they stand unchallenged, is actually *indoctrination;* but it passes for education and always has.

The full measure of Dewey's success can be appreciated when we consider that anyone who has been through the American school system who still does not believe in evolution today is automatically labeled "uneducated," "reactionary," or "religious" in a derogatory sense.

Yet the fact is that contemporary scientists quietly discarded Darwin's ideas years ago. We, the public, were left in the dark about this retreat, to be sure. Still, when word gets around that the theory of evolution is in no way substantiated by science, that it is, from a scientific standpoint, an unsubstantiated hypothesis, the taxpayers (parents in particular) will demand that the educational system and its Dewey*istic* philosophy be radically changed. These new reformers will be looking for specific causes and specific solutions. When they look they will find that one root source of today's problems lies with the fact that the teachers have lost virtually all legal authority over their students, particularly in the junior and senior high schools.

Imagine the impotence of a construction boss if he could do nothing about an employee who refused to work, or refused to follow orders and plans, or refused to be civil and cooperative to a degree that was detrimental to the completion of the project at hand! Imagine the policeman, the fireman, the judge, and so forth, without legal authority to carry out his duties!

In the materialistic, live-for-the-moment modern world that indoctrination in evolutionary thought has bequeathed us, there can be little wonder that students view their lessons as merely bothersome nonsense and their teachers as total or partial fools. But the debunking of evolutionary theory coupled with the restoration of teacher authority will quickly improve the climate for both teaching and learning.

Specifically, reformers will certainly note that a second root source of today's public education problems lies with the radical shift in religious emphasis that has occurred since the Supreme Court outlawed any mention of religion in 1962. After this decision, a new faith took over which demanded a great deal more of a student's time than had the religion it supplanted. The new object of devotion, evolution, based its belief completely and without reservation upon faith. The new faith was in science, but it was no less a faith for *there is not one shred of evidence of any sort in any scientific field that proves evolution.* This fact—that evolution is a religion based strictly on faith (faith in the *demonstrably* impossible, it should be emphasized)—must be hammered home by all who want public education to survive.

When the Supreme Court acts again, it must surely consider the injustice and unconstitutionality of daily perpetuation at taxpayers' expense of a religious myth based on faith alone. Hopefully the court will act before the students are further misled and the schools descend still deeper into anarchy and chaos.*

A third specific problem which reformers will note has to do with the fact that secondary school codes and rules nowadays are primarily dictated by students. This frequently means virtually no rules and virtually no en-

---

*An excellent account of the effects of teaching evolution in public schools can be found in *Earth's Most Challenging Mysteries* by Reginald Daly (The Craig Press, Box 13, Nutley, NJ 07110), pp. 386-396.

forcement. There can be little wonder that students think they know more than parents and teachers. They—not the adults—decide what they will wear, what music will be played in the cafeteria, what can be gotten away with on attendance, homework, attitude, course selection, and general behavior. Thus have Dewey's child-centered notions succeeded in making a mockery of the learning process in far too many classrooms.

Told in science class that they are just animals, students proceed to act as if this were so in other classes, at home, and in their social lives. Seeing no purpose to life, they become selfish and churlish. It is a pitiful thing to see so many youths so rudderless, so loveless—so blameless, basically. The situation is desperate in many urban schools. The time to expose evolution as a myth, and thereby begin to restore dignity and purpose to the learning process is now.

Specifically, concerned parents must reassert themselves in the educational process. They must reassert their authority at home. They must decide whether their children deserve cars, motorcycles, and unrestricted hours. They must help. Those parents who altruistically championed the revolution in student rights must surely see the folly of that path by now! This does doubly for many teachers who enthusiastically helped create the Frankenstein that now threatens their sanity and their jobs, not to mention the continuance of organized society. When evolution was "true" and "God was dead," this madness in the schools and other types of madness made a crazy kind of sense. Once the evolution myth is exposed, however, and a Creator logically proven, rational people—teachers, students, everybody—can shift out of reverse gear mentally, and get into forward gear. Education is one place where this shift is urgently needed.

There will be other things that parents and other adults will insist upon, no doubt. Generally, these demands will be aimed at undoing the Spockian permissiveness that was a logical outgrowth of Dewey's educational philosophy, a philosophy that built its "new logic" upon the evolutionary myth. Adults will demand and must demand that the control of schools be taken out of the hands of students.

There can be no doubt that parents will want authoritative discipline reinstated. They will want academic standards tightened up. They will want grades to count again, and they will want them to be worked for. They will want dress for students—and to some degree, for faculty—to be prescribed. They will want the emphasis on college for everyone decreased somewhat and emphasis on vocational schools increased somewhat. They will want a counterrevolution.

The pendulum, in short, will swing back. It may go too far, but there are few today who would not find reaction preferable to the impossible situation which exists in many American public schools at the present time. The widespread disregard for necessary levels of authority and discipline, the shallow life goals, insufficient funds resulting in shorter terms and overcrowdedness, teacher strikes, racial tensions and clashes, and myriad other problems small and large, have put American education in the critical ward. To recover, reaction is necessary.

But better discipline and more rigid standards may well fail too if students can't be infused with a positive attitude toward life. Present difficulties stem from the implicit question in the minds of the young: Is there escape from the seeming meaninglessness of life? Name *any* subject, *any* endeavor, and students know a good argument that can be made against wasting their time with that subject or endeavor. The depth of this nihilism (rejection of all truths and moral principles) in so many youngsters is the tragedy of our time. Evolution, we maintain, is its root cause because evolution takes away the idealistic reasons for life and substitutes materialistic ones. With evolution flushed out of curriculum philosophy, however, we can look forward confidently to the restoration of purposeful life goals in the schools. If we only have the wisdom to restrain those who would go too far, we will yet come up with a school system that will provide our children with the tools and the values needed for living their three score and ten years fully and happily.

The transformation of the "logic of knowledge" caused by the theory of evolution, must simply go through another transformation when that theory is debunked. Education—American and otherwise—needs a new philosopher, one with the genius and energy of Dewey, but one motivated by yet another—and perhaps final—new "logic of knowledge."

Freud's Impact on Modern Behavior

Friedrich Nietzsche, the German philosopher of the late nineteenth century, carried evolutionary thought to its apogee in his cry: "God is dead. We have killed Him . . . with our rationality and our science." Nietzsche was read by people who influenced thought and action. The same was true of John Dewey.

Jean Paul Sartre and other existentialists served the same negative cause, as did Bertrand Russell in his way, and, for that matter, H. L. Mencken in his. All of these people, plus the scientists quoted in this book, furthered the cause of evolution. Presumably, *they all acted in good faith*, directing their talents to a theory alleged to have the full support of science.

Over and above these, however, stand three men whose ideas have become the intellectual bedrock of our century: Charles Darwin, Karl Marx, and Sigmund Freud. Of Darwin, we have said enough. A later chapter is dedicated to Marx. It is to Freud that we now turn.

Sigmund Freud's impact on our culture, our thinking, is almost beyond measure, as the following assessments show:

> Sigmund Freud's name is as cardinal in the history of human thought as Charles Darwin's.[19]
>
> Few others in the history of the world have had a more profound influence on the way man thinks about himself.[20]
>
> The very intellectual air we breathe has been infused with Freud's categories of thought.[21]
>
> In the wide area of experience covered by the Humanities and Social Sciences it is difficult to find a single discipline that is not indebted to Freud's theories.[22]
>
> Probably no scientist has ever had so strong and so wide-spread an influence upon literature.[23]
>
> No other thinker in modern times has had a comparable effect upon so many branches of knowledge.[24]

As with philosophers, Freud influenced even those who never read him—people who have little or no interest in psychology or psychiatry. His theories simply became part and parcel of our heritage. Whether we know his theories or not, whether we have read his books or not, we have—all of us—been affected, in one way or another, by Freud's revolutionary conception of man.

As a medical student, writing about what shaped his philosophy, Freud said:

> The theory of Darwin in its beginning at that time attracted me mightily because it promised to advance tremendously a knowledge of the world.[25]

Freud was influenced both by Darwin and by Goethe:

> I know that the rendering of Goethe's beautiful essay *Die Natur* at a popular lecture led me to decide shortly before graduation to matriculate in medicine.[26]

Johann Wolfgang von Goethe, the German poet, dramatist, and novelist, was also gifted in science. He conceived a theory of evolution as early as 1784. His work, along with that of Buffon and Lamarck, paved the way to Darwin's theory.

In his very thorough book on Freud, Wittels, a psychoanalyst himself, and an exponent of Freudian theory a generation ago, says of Goethe's influence on the young Sigmund:

> Freud admits that Goethe exercised a decisive influence upon his youth.[27]

This gives us some idea of Freud's admiration for Goethe and Darwin, both evolutionists. We mention this to point out that the theory of evolution was instrumental in shaping Freud's view of man. The full measure of this fact can best be judged from Freud's own words.

> Man is not different from, or better than, the animals. . . .[28]

The present development of mankind seems to me to demand no other explanation than that of the animals. . . .[29]

As Rushdoony makes clear in his excellent monograph, *Freud:*

> [Freud] was an evolutionary scientist, and he recognized that evolution was fundamental to his perspective.[30]

Not only did Freud base his entire stock of notions on the conviction that man is an evolved animal, he stubbornly held to the Lamarckian concept of acquired characteristics, a view that Huxley and almost all sophisticated evolutionists have disowned. But:

> For Freud the issue was simple: invalidate Lamarck, and you invalidate evolution.[31]

It is a natural step from being a pure evolutionist to being an atheist. Some may not follow that pattern (they may compromise), but it is natural. Another step in the pattern is to place one's trust in science, the *real* God substitute. Freud followed this pattern perfectly. He wrote a book, *The Future of an Illusion,* describing religions as "wish fulfillments" and God as a "father substitute." In the last paragraph, he makes his position quite clear:

> No, science is no illusion. But it would be an illusion to suppose that we could get anywhere else what it cannot give us.[32]

An evolutionist and an atheist, Freud believed that no answers could be found outside of science.

He then started his approach to psychoanalysis, to the scientific investigation of man. In the briefest of terms, his theory, as it is generally understood, can be reduced to this: Sex is the prime motivating force of humankind.* This theory hit the Victorian era with the force of an explosion.

Freud, nevertheless, in time was able to overcome both outside objections and the resistance of others in his profession. As early as the last part of the last century, he began to attract the attention of students of psychoanalysis. Several came to Vienna to study his methods, among them, Karl Jung and Alfred Adler. Both men soon disagreed with critical parts of Freud's theory, however, and they finally broke away to form psychoanalytical schools of their own. Jung, for his part, "denied the sexuality of the libido,"[33] while Adler "denied the unconscious."[34] Since the sexuality of the libido and the reality of the unconscious are key features of Freudian theory, it can be said that Freud lost his star pupils because they couldn't go along with two of his main premises. They, and others who have rejected key aspects of Freudianism, have proven what most people still don't know, namely, that psychoanalysis is not a science. If it were, psychoanalysts would not have different opinions about the same phenomena. In this sense, psychiatry is in a similar position to evolutionary science and Marxism. All three lay claim to a scientific method,

---

*Some idea of where a psychologist's diagnosis can begin if he is sufficiently convinced of man's pure animality, can be seen in this laundry list of Freudian nomenclature: unconscious behavior; the id, ego, and superego; the Oedipus complex; infantile sexuality; word associations; father hatred or worship or substitution; dream analysis; the libido; hypnotism; totemism and taboos; penis envy; wish-fulfillment; sublimation; sadism and masochism; phallic symbols; the pleasure principle; the death instinct; the Primary Horde; homosexuality; incest; bisexuality; anal eroticism; exhibitionism; megalomania; narcissism; neurosis; paranoia; erotomania; psychosis; fetishism; inferiority feelings; the castration complex; anxiety; hysteria; etc., etc., etc.

whereas actually they hang on a set of assumptions which are rejected by many completely rational people.

To be sure, psychology is categorized as a social science, and not a natural science, and, therefore, is not expected to be "very" scientific. It is in the social sciences, as we have seen, that the influence of Freudian psychoanalytic theory has been most keenly felt. Sociology, economics, history, government, anthropology have all geared many of their interpretations to accommodate the hot breath of the Freudian subconscious. It is interesting too that all the social sciences lately have tried to copy the "real" sciences, by using "pseudomathematical decorations," as Andreski calls them, to make their work look scientific and thus increase their drives—to be "gods" too. As far as psychological pretentions to being scientific go, a new book concludes that

> ... much of what passes as scientific study of human behavior boils down to sorcery....[35]

This type of criticism indicates that it is not just the natural sciences that are beginning to be scrutinized and criticized for going beyond their ken, but that the social sciences (and arts and humanities) can be expected to be seen running up distress signals too. The reason? They are all distorted to one degree or another by their considerable dependence on interpretations that have grown out of the thinking of Darwin, Marx, and Freud.

As this statement indicates, Darwin's theory was recognized by both Freud and Marx as being of central importance to their concepts of man and civilization:

> Freud, like Marx, sees the development of man in evolutionary terms.... Freud's picture of the *development of the human race* resembles ... that of individual development.... He sees primitive

man as one who gives full satisfaction to all his instincts, and also to those perverse instincts which are part of primitive sexuality....[36]

In a book titled *Freud and Marx* author Reuben Osborn shows several similarities in the two men's thinking, particularly as regards the supposed sexual brutishness of primitive societies. In fact, Osborn believes that

> the best point of departure for a study of the relationship between Freudian and Marxian theories is a consideration of primitive society, for here they have much in common.[37]

Friedrich Engels, co-author with Marx of *The Communist Manifesto,* was, like Marx and Freud, fully convinced that man's nature was animistic, due to the fact that he evolved from lower animals. Engels, who was quite intrigued with the idea of group marriages and communal living among primitive peoples, wrote in his book, *The Origin of the Family,* which is " ... now required reading in many women's studies courses"[38]:

> All the forms of the group marriage known to us are accompanied by such peculiarly complicated circumstances that they of necessity point to a preceding simpler form of sexual intercourse and, hence, in the last instance to a period of unrestricted sexual intercourse corresponding to a transition from the animal to man.[39]

The attitudes of these men certainly contributed to the "free love" platforms of the early communists in Russia and elsewhere. Indeed, these attitudes, amplified and dispersed under a variety of labels all traceable to Freudian sexual concepts, go far toward explaining the "anything goes" sexual revolution now cresting in most advanced societies in our own time.

It doesn't matter that Freud has been out of vogue in some psychiatric circles for fifteen or twenty years. His effect on modern beliefs about sexual matters has been the primary force in the sexual revolution, nonetheless. There are direct connections from Freudianism to increased pornography, to attacks on the family unit, to soaring divorce rates, to gay lib, to almost casual abortions, and to other exhortations to make sexuality the be-all and end-all of life. The fact that this emphasis causes far more anxiety and frustration than the pleasure and freedom it seems to offer is explained away as just another aspect of "reality" that "stable" people have to accept as the world gets rid of its old God-centered morality and adjusts to the "truth" of nihilism. And for this advice society applauds and some people pay fifty dollars an hour!

The collapse of evolutionary theory cannot fail, however, to bring about the collapse of other theories that branch off from it. Freudian psychology in all its ramifications is one of those branches. The whole process can be visualized as a tree trunk with branches—something like the evolutionists once used themselves. But this tree trunk is labeled "The Truth." There are several large limbs each of which represent man's efforts to apply "The Truth" to the world about him. There are limbs for the religions of the world, each with branches for the different sects. There are broken stubs of limbs, for dead religions and gods, among them Zeus, Osiris, Quetzalcoatl. And there is one large limb growing abnormally near the ground—the furthest away from the pinnacle of the trunk—which is God. This is the limb where man has strayed the furthest from "The Truth." This is the limb of evolution. One of its prominent branches is Freudian psychology, which in turn has its offshoots of pornography, communal sex, family breakdown, incest, homosexuality, and other encouragements to pure sexuality inherent in Freudianism.

Man now has the scientific and logical knowledge to saw this limb off. When the limb dies, so will its branches and their offshoots.*

But we must leave further expansion of these specifics to others, and briefly concentrate here on an overview of Freud's role in what might be called three of the main keys to twentieth-century thought. The keys are: 1) evolutionary theory demanded a new logic; 2) Marxism was that new logic; 3) Freudianism was recognized as a useful way of bringing about that new logic. In *Freud and Marx,* we read of the need for a new logic:

> But in the face of the growing knowledge that the higher and more complex forms of existence were related to the lower and more simple, that what had been considered a divine act of creation was really the product of a lengthy process of evolution, there arose a need for a logic which expressed these facts.[40]

---

*Another large branch on the limb of evolution is Marxian communism. Among its offshoots are Maoism, Fidelism, Titoism, Trotskyism, Stalinism. On the other side of the limb but still basing their truths on evolution are vestiges of Hitler's Nazism, Mussolini's Fascism. There are branches for all man's endeavors that have grown out of the evolution concept of truth. The arts are there, with twigs for abstract music, painting, literature, architecture, drama, et al. The natural sciences form a branch with twigs. So do the social sciences and philosophy and the humanities. Little has escaped this massive growth on the tree of truth. Yet the limb was fed by the trunk ... and reasonably so, for man has learned new truths about his capacity for self-deception. He has come to grips with evil and with beauty that he would not have known, with truths about his capabilities and capacities that would have been missed, if the world had remained as it was in 1750 or 1850. The triumph of evolution and its coming downfall could well be the grandest and last lesson that man needs to show him the folly of ignoring God as the pinnacle of The Truth.

The Marxist revolutionaries were possessors of the new logic, but they early recognized that "the problem of socialism is not only economic, but psychological."[41] The question they had to ask themselves, the Marxists knew, was:

> How can we, in a given set of circumstances, get the workers feeling and thinking in terms of revolutionary activity?[42]

Osborn, a Marxist theoretician in the 30s, had an interesting answer:

> Painstaking investigation into the fundamental psychological processes which interact with the world of economics is called for. Freud, courageous pioneer in this work, deserves place with Darwin and Marx in the revolutionary discoveries he has made concerning man. Whoever wishes to maintain a claim to being a revolutionary, in outlook and deed, must not only master the Marxist laws of social development, but must also embrace, as an essential part of Marxian outlook, the Freudian dynamics of psychological phenomena.[43]

There is abundant evidence that this advice has been carried out to a remarkable degree: that it has been, in all truth, carried out on a level so subtle and even so *unconscious* most of the time, and yet so thorough, that it is all but impossible for anyone to clearly pinpoint its antecedents or its direction. Yet, *it has been done!* "Freudian dynamics" and the Marxian view together constitute the "new logic" that motivates millions today: a new logic that will become irrelevant with the death of the theory of evolution, upon which it all rests.

The temptation is strong to go further into the

theme of Freudian influence on Marxist thought and how both owe so much to the evolutionary concept of man. The connections are all there. Among the psychologists-philosophers there is Wilhelm Reich, more Freudian than Freud, attempting "to politicise sex"[44] as he put it. There is Norman Brown saying that the elusive answers to behavior are to be found in the "social organization which marks the transition from ape to man."[45] There is Herbert Marcuse ending up by advocating "nice" violence and undemocratic privileges for minority revolutionaries.[46] Or, to take just one other avenue of influence, there is even Robert Audrey, who writes of a sort of souped-up Freudianism in his books, saying: "As an evolutionist, I am skeptical of established American Anthropology." Having thus stated his position, Audrey proceeds with a two-page review of a book which deals with a one-man "scientific" mission to observe the behavior of an African tribe. The book is presumably being reviewed so that readers can get the author's important message that, under certain circumstances, man is pure evil;[47] a message all too common to evolutionists with a Freudian bent; a message which—unwittingly or not—serves only to debase man.

We will leave this section with a little test that will permit *you* to read *Freudian* interpretations into different examples of behavior, examples which you can rate on a scale of one to five. Number one is normal; number two is eccentric but okay; number three is definitely "funny" but probably harmless; number four is sick; maybe curable, maybe not; number five is "bananas"—no hope.

It's simple. Just read the short example of an actual behavior pattern, and apply your own Freudian interpretation. Ready? Here are ten examples taken from actual psychological records: Circle the number you think fits the case. (Remember that 1 = normal; 2 = eccentric but okay; 3 = definitely "funny" but probably harmless; 4 = sick, maybe curable, maybe not; 5 = "bananas"—no hope.)

Case Number 1: A middle-aged professional man admits to being afraid of trains. He experiences great anxiety when he knows he must travel by train (which is frequently). He will not travel alone, and insists on being at the station one hour ahead of time. (1 - 2 - 3 - 4 - 5)

Case Number 2: A small child has a death wish for a younger brother. The brother dies. (1 - 2 - 3 - 4 - 5)

Case Number 3: A successful medical doctor, in good health, aged forty, confesses that he has stopped having sexual relations with his wife, and can only be stimulated sexually by perverse fantasies. (1 - 2 - 3 - 4 - 5)

Case Number 4: An academic celebrity of mature years describes inability to maintain friendships with colleagues; speaks of latent homosexuality in himself and others; admits to stealing an important concept from a good friend and associate; has fainted outright on two occasions, when facing colleagues. (1 - 2 - 3 - 4 - 5)

Case Number 5: A creative scientist believes an intellectual elite should run society; practices authoritarianism himself. (1 - 2 - 3 - 4 - 5)

Case Number 6: A boy, aged sixteen; lives in a large household with his aging father, young mother, and seven half brothers who are as old as his mother. Boy shows intense mother fixation, but refuses to discuss his anxieties. (1 - 2 - 3 - 4 - 5)

Case Number 7: An assistant professor in a European university earned promotion after seventeen years only with outside help. Same professor successfully assures his future through mysterious organization called "The Seven Rings" of which he is the unchallenged leader. (1 - 2 - 3 - 4 - 5)

Case Number 8: A noted author ignores wife's wishes; refuses to allow her to accompany him on trips; buys house without consulting her; is unsociable at dinner table, usually brings a newly purchased statuette to the table for a companion. (1 - 2 - 3 - 4 - 5)

Case Number 9: A teenage student engages in intense hero worship of Hannibal and William the Conqueror. Later identifies himself with Michelangelo; forms a fixation upon Moses and appears to believe he either was Moses or is a new Moses. (1 - 2 - 3 - 4 - 5)

Case Number 10: A celebrated refugee in his eighties maintains that reason is the only guide in life; maintains that feelings and emotions are per se irrational, and hence inferior to thought. Maintains that common sense is of little value. (1 - 2 - 3 - 4 - 5)

The way you scored these cases doesn't much matter. One could argue convincingly for more than one choice in most of the cases. The interesting fact is that all ten cases are about the same person. You guessed it: Sigmund Freud!

The vine that grew out of his tangled brain had its taproot in evolutionary thought. When that taproot is killed, the vine too must die. As with biology the core of psychology and psychiatry will be discredited with the collapse of evolutionary theory. This will mean that new directions—with God as the core—will have to be found if these professions are to survive the collapse of evolutionary theory.

Communism

After he read *The Origin of Species,* Karl Marx, the

recognized founder of communism, wrote to Freidrich Engels:

> ... this is the book which contains the basis in natural history for our view.[48]

A year later (1861) Marx was still writing of the unexpected good fortune in finding so powerful an ally in the natural sciences for his own theories in the social sciences. To Lassalle, a revolutionary, he exulted that God—in the natural sciences, at least—had been given "the death blow" by Darwin.[49] He further wrote:

> Darwin's book is very important and serves me as a basis for the class struggle in history.[50]

A few years later (1867) Marx finished the first volume of his major work and, as mentioned elsewhere, wanted to dedicate it to Darwin, whose theory he realized could be critically important to the success of his communist brand of socialism. The inseparable nature of socialism—whatever its type—and evolutionary theory was recognized by Spengler. As he made clear:

> Socialism and Darwinism are only artificially and on the surface separable.[51]

One thing that Marx and Engels seemed to agree upon completely, one thing they never forgot, was the fact that communism was to be based on a strictly materialistic (no God) view of man and the universe. This is the same view basically that the theory of evolution seemed to confirm scientifically. Then, as the theory of evolution succeeded in becoming the dominant view in the natural sciences, nothing could be more reasonable than to expect that other new thinking based on the same view of man would also succeed. So Freud succeeded in changing psychology and psychiatry.

Dewey changed education. Art changed. So did philosophy, music, and literature. Sociology converted totally. Hardly anything escaped the "new logic." Once this is fully understood, it is possible to understand fully something else that is extremely important, namely, that *communism is just the new way of thinking—the new logic—applied to economics and politics.*

The continuing success in all the other fields made it possible for communism to eventually succeed somewhere, somehow. Indeed, *Marx's chief claim to fame should be that he designed a political and economic system for a Godless world before Darwin's theory made that view of the world fashionable.* Marx's ideas would never have gained a large following, nor would they have been applied, in a world where the intelligentsia was still God-centered. It simply could not have happened. Nor, of course, would the ideas of Freud, Nietzsche, Dewey, and other champions of the "new logic" have succeeded with a God-centered intelligentsia. Thus, even though evolutionary theory began to make an impact on certain intellectuals in the mid-1700s, it took Darwin and scientific respectability a generation to establish a beachhead in the universities, two generations to wrest control of several strategic disciplines, three generations to crush and silence intellectual opposition in the universities and even the urban high schools, and four generations to capture a good part of the literate masses of the world and indoctrinate them with the "new truth."

Now, to be sure, Marx formulated his ideas before Darwin published *The Origin of Species.* Nevertheless, he met with nothing but failure until Darwin's theory penetrated and altered the basic view of man's nature in the minds of succeeding generations of intellectuals. Until this change was achieved there were never more than a handful of people who took his ideas seriously. At his death in 1883, Marx's ideas had made virtually no impact anywhere. Such was the fruit of almost forty years of effort. His ideas—openly atheistic as they were—simply were not geared to a time when virtually all the masses and most of the intellectuals believed in a power beyond man. But at his death the forces were already growing strong in certain circles which would effectively undermine a belief in God. When that was sufficiently accomplished, and only then, communism had a chance of succeeding. Darwinism was the main agent in bringing about this change. It did not father Marx's child, but without its success, communism would have continued to be a puny wretch of an idea unable to stand alone. In other words, *the success of Marxism is inextricably linked to the success of Darwinism.* Engels, without knowing what was to come, wisely recognized this close connection in his oration delivered at Marx's graveside. He said:

> Just as Darwin discovered the law of organic evolution in human history, so Marx discovered the law of evolution in human history.[52]

It is also evident in this quotation that Engels considered Marx a scientist and Marxism (communism) a science. Notice that he says "law" of evolution in both cases, an extremely unscientific label for two totally unproven, and totally unprovable, guesses.

This sort of claim to being scientific, however grossly unfounded it had to be, was, nevertheless, crucially important to the growth of communism. Marxist theory, in fact, rode to success on this claim in a world that more and more was turning to science for answers to all things. As you have seen, the realization that science has failed as a God-substitute is just now causing a swelling tide of reaction. In two, three, or four years this will be a full tide. When the tide goes out, communism will be one of many things caught in the undertow.

Look at it this way: the whole idea of science is based on order. Without order, no predictions can be made. Without predictions, one can only guess, or wish, or hope that something will develop in a given way. This guessing, wishing, or hoping is hardly what we would want to label scientific.

Yet, there was no order or system in Marx's time which gave him grounds to assert *as a scientist* that communist-socialism was destined to be *the* world system. There were no examples in history from which he could draw such a conclusion. He just did it. He drew conclusions and made predictions out of a flimsy hypothesis (guess) and it has been called "scientific" ever since. The absurdity of his whole procedure was perfectly obvious in his own time in a world which, for all its errors, had not forgotten the distinction between guesses and science. Only after Darwin, Nietzsche, Freud, and others had succeeded in making such pseudoscientific guesses the new God-substitute, only then could the economic and political solutions of Marx be entertained. Absurd solutions had to wait on an absurd world. Then they could be called "scientific."

So *science* was the magic word in those days, and has remained so until the present, a fact that cannot be repeated too often. All ideas that were labeled "scientific" by a few "scientists" stood to prosper in such a climate. As Barzun, who spells all this out in detail, puts it:

> In insisting upon group violence for alleged economic ends *under the aegis of would-be scientific theories,* Marx was in step with all the cultural

forces of his age and fastened his grip on the future[53] (our emphasis).

Communism, then, was to benefit greatly in the twentieth century by the fact that people—university people in particular—looked upon Marx's theories as something scientific, that is, as something infallible or very nearly so. Yet, to be legitimately called "scientific," an idea or process must have some standards of reliability, some rate of predictability. Marxism rates very low as a science by these criteria. All, or virtually all, of Marx's major predictions not only failed to work out, the *opposite* of what he forecast more commonly came to pass. He (with Engels) was sure, for example, that the 1848 uprisings in Europe were sounding the death knell of capitalism. In actual fact, of course, reaction settled back over the continent and Marx had to flee to England. Looking back in 1895, Engels admitted:

> History has proved us, and all who thought like us, wrong. It has made clear that the state of economic development on the Continent at that time was not, by a long way, ripe for the elimination of capitalist production....[54]

Then too, Marx's publications were supposed to spark a communist movement. Instead, in 1859, his *Critique of Political Economy* was stillborn.[55] Eight laborious years later, the partially completed *Das Kapital* was published and studiously ignored. Marx predicted that communism would succeed first in Germany, then perhaps England. He was quite explicit in saying that the revolution had to occur in a highly industrialized state where there were plenty of exploited factory workers. The two main communist successes have, of course, been in Russia and China, both 85 percent agricultural at the time of their revolutions. Thus Russia and China stand as conspicuous examples of the nonpredictability of Marx's nonscience.

Marx predicted that the only way workers would get better pay and conditions was through violent overthrow of the ownership class. This hasn't happened in the United States, Canada, Western Europe, Japan, Latin America (except for Cuba), and other places where workers' unions have gained benefits that are not matched in communist countries. Scientist Marx didn't allow for this development.

Marx stands today in a position very much like that of Darwin and Freud. Practically *everything* he said which was taken as gospel and started a movement in his name has been *proven* unsound. If this is what we must call scientific, then science has indeed reached its nadir as an aid to guiding man's well-being.

There three men, whose work has led the way in a worldwide transvaluation of values, all based their theories on the idea that life, the world, and the universe are accidents without meaning or purpose. Man, as they viewed him, was another animal whose needs were to be determined with his animal nature foremost in mind. With Darwin's "scientific" guesses *entirely* disproven (and that of latter day evolutionists on the brink of being similarly discounted), *all systems, teachings, and plans based on man as an evolved animal must be reassessed.*

When this one thing, this reassessment, is undertaken by leaders in virtually all fields of endeavor, then the incredible depth of man's deception and the more incredible depth of his efforts to adjust to that deception will keep all of us laughing—sometimes through tears, no doubt—for a very long time.

Consider again Marx and communism. Only a civilization becoming progressively irrational and driven ever deeper into a Darwinian nonworld by Nietzsche, Freud, Dewey, and others, could ever have taken this man and his ideas seriously.

Look at both the man and the system and you will see what is true but rarely emphasized.

Marx, the scientist, was a very suspicious man; paranoid, we would say today. He saw spies everywhere. In choosing other German refugees to work with him in the library of the British Museum, he screened each one carefully and personally to determine whether they had the qualities he sought. His test consisted of feeling, examining, and noting the bumps on each volunteer's head as he gave them his craniology test. Yes, Marx was a phrenologist. That is to say, he judged people's mental abilities, their loyalty, and other traits by the conformation of their skulls, the bumps on their heads.

Marx, the economist, had a world economic plan. Basically it called for the confiscation of property by the state and redistribution according to needs. No such plan *had* ever worked on anything but the smallest scale for very short periods of time, and no such plan *has* ever worked since it was devised by Marx. Nevertheless, Marx said it was a scientific, historical fact and that such was to be the wave of the future. And (understandably, because that is what has been taught) a lot of people believe it is scientific, that it is an historical fact, and that it is to be the wave of the future. Such unfounded faith will be impossible once the cornerstone of Marx's philosophy—a materialistic world with accidentally evolved mankind—is undermined.

Engels called all this the negation of the negation, a meaningless, and thus strangely appropriate, designation. (Engel's name, it should be remembered, is virtually interchangeable with Marx's as they were "one of one soul"[56] according to Liebknecht who knew them both well.)

We can use *A, B,* and *C* to explain the negation of the negation. Letter *A* represents primitive man's supposed communal property arrangements. (Engel's evidence for this is *very* thin, being based almost entirely on one man's account of his years spent with an Indian tribe.) Anyway, along came *B* (private property) and negated *A*. Now, Engels said, the time is at hand when *C* (communal property owned by the state) is going to negate *B.*

All of this is a hypothesis (guess) of course, because there simply was no observable evidence that could lead one to draw such conclusions. Indeed such evidence as there was then (experimental communist settlements such as New Harmony) were conspicuous failures. In recent years dozens of communal living experiments have stagnated and collapsed and now stand only as final evidence of the folly of this economic and social arrangement.

But the evidence in communist countries since then is even more damning to the hypothesis. In those countries *C* (state ownership) is maintained only by the strictest enforcement of national law. Even so, every time the restraints are lifted, *C* reverts to *B* as surely as water seeks its own level. The Soviet Union was forced as early as the New Economic Policy of 1921 to abandon important aspects of plan *C.* They now permit ownership of small acreage and sales for profit of certain products and numerous other capitalist-type incentives. While the "socialization of the soil" in the Soviet Union has culminated in almost comical inefficiency and the necessity of buying tremendous quantities of grain from several capitalist countries (including one-fourth of the 1972 U.S.

crop!), the mini-private farms that are permitted, produce prodigiously. Writer Hughes reports:

> Today those private plots make up only 3 percent of the cultivated land. [Nevertheless] ... they furnish fully one quarter of all Soviet farm output.[57]

It is doubtful if the Soviets could return to *C* even with force. If they did, they would either starve or be forced to buy another quarter of their needs from systems which Marx and Engels consigned to the ash heap of history over a century ago. All other communist experiments have had similar frustrations in agriculture and other areas of the economy. State ownership of all property is not efficient, much less popular, and cannot be maintained without coercion. It is the opposite of the scientific reality that Marx and Engels tried to make it. Castro never fulfills his sugar quota and he never will. Russia cannot feed its people from state run farms now, and it will not be able to in the future.

After a decade and a half of *C*, Mao Tse-tung staged a cultural revolution in China, still trying to stamp out the ideas associated with *B* which constantly threatened his nearly pure brand of state ownership. *Without dictatorial coercion, in other words, communist economics reverts to capitalist economics.* This is the iron law of economics as indicated by actual experiment. This law makes nonsense of all communist efforts to label themselves scientific.

All of this does not mean that 100 percent Adam Smith capitalism is desirable or even workable. It is neither desirable nor workable.

Nor does it mean that socialism has nothing to offer. On the contrary, in light of the evidence, it can be said that a 30 percent or so public sector (*C*) is a useful and beneficial level of government interference in an economy. As such, it is something positive that can be attributed to practical socialism. Beyond a 50 percent public sector, however, gets to be irrational and unscientific, as the many exotic troubles in Sweden, England, Uruguay, and many other countries will attest. As one's economics become increasingly irrational (Marxist), the door is then open to other irrationalities based on Darwinian-Freudian-Marxian views of man as an animal. (The breakdown of the family—recommended, you recall, by Engels in his book *The Origin of the Family*—is but one of the tragic consequences of irrational and unscientific Marxism that is taking an unmeasurable but grim emotional toll, especially among the young, in northern Europe and the United States.)

Marx, the economist, lived in abject poverty most of his adult life. So destitute was his family that five of his seven children died, most of them, apparently, from malnutrition and other complications related to their destitute condition. Marx, who steadfastly refused to seek a paying job (aside from a pittance for his *New York Herald Tribune* pieces), was no stranger to the pawnshop. He was kept going financially all his life primarily by Engels, whose father was a capitalist manufacturer.

Some appreciation of Marx's ineptitude at running his own domestic economy can be seen in Rühle's summary:

> Throughout his life, he was hard up. He was ridiculously ineffectual in his endeavours to cope with the economic needs of his household and his family; and his incapacity in monetary matters involved him in an endless series of struggles and catastrophes. He was always in debt; was incessantly being dunned by creditors, persecuted by

usurers, drained by bloodsuckers. Half his household goods were always at the pawnshop. His budget defied all attempts to set it in order. His bankruptcy was chronic. The thousands upon thousands which Engels handed over to him melted away in his fingers like snow.[58]

It may be protested that Marx's genius was too far above these ordinary facts of life for him to cope with the everyday question of earning a living; that such a person can't be judged by conventional values, and so on. On the other hand, it can be argued that such a mental giant ought to be able to figure out how to keep food on the table while he formulated his abstract theories. Marx had a head start in life, after all, having gotten his Ph.D. by the age of twenty-four. But again, one must not judge everyone by the same measure. Perhaps Marx's dedication to the cause of justice and humanity kept him too busy to earn even a minimal living; that indeed he suffered (and his family suffered) selflessly and willingly to help bring about a better world. It can even be said that such devotion to a cause is the more admirable still because Marx expected no reward in an afterlife for his dead children, suffering wife, or himself.

An argument can be made along these lines, to be sure.

Nevertheless, it is an argument that holds very little water.

One can establish beyond challenge, for example, that Marx was an intolerant boor; that he stole most of his important ideas from others; that he produced remarkably little in a forty-year career uninterrupted by steady employment; that he was a failure as a leader of the Communist International; that he was the opposite of scientific; that his whole reputation as the founder of a humane system leading to a bright and shining world is grossly misleading.

Some of these traits have been shown. Consider these additions briefly. As to Marx's character, for example, we learn that he was a typical authoritarian,[59] "arrogant, self-conceited, dogmatic, disputatious, irritable."[60] Carl Schurz, who later had a brilliant and varied career in America, knew Marx during the 1848-49 uprisings. He labeled him "insufferably arrogant," and said that he allowed no one to contradict him.[61] Mazzini, the Italian nationalist, said of Marx: "Hatred outweighs love in his heart...."[62] Bakunin, whom Marx succeeded as head of the Communist International, called Marx "vain and jealous," among other things.[63] Rühle, who strives to give a balanced portrait of Marx, nevertheless notes the man's extremely uncooperative and overbearing nature:

> He, Marx alone, was in possession of the true doctrine.... With contemptuous wrath, with bitter mockery and profound hostility, he rejected all other opinions, fought against all other convictions than his own, persecuted all ideas that had not originated in his own brain. For him, there was no wisdom except his own.... His system was Allah, and he was its prophet.[64]

Though born Jewish (his family converted to Christianity when he was six), Marx attacked Jews as well as Christians. One of his antagonists he labeled a "Jewish Nigger."[65]

Whether the charge of outright plagiarism is fair can be judged by a glance at some of the evidence. This evidence shows that Marx "borrowed" Hegel's dialectic method and altered it to suit his purposes. In varying degrees, Marx "borrowed" from Fourier, Proudhon, and

Backunin without giving credit. From Saint Simon he "borrowed" the class-war idea which is central to his whole philosophy. For "The Communist Manifesto" (a forty-page pamphlet) Marx required the co-authorship of Engels who outlined the statement for him. (Engels did a lot of the actual writing for which the world gives Marx credit.) Moreover, Victor Considerant had said essentially the same things in his "Manifesto de la Democracie"[66] written before "The Communist Manifesto," a fact Marx failed to report. Take away Considerant's contribution, says Dr. Jacques Barzun, and all that remains of "The Communist Manifesto" is dogma and a call to action.[67] Marx even signed pieces sent to the *New York Tribune* for years, many of which were completely written by Engels.

In September 1872, Marx took over the direction of the Communist International. By September 1873

> Marx had to admit . . . that the International had collapsed. . . . When Bakunin died on July 1, 1876, no trace of the Marxian International remained.[68]

One seeks in vain for evidence that Karl Marx was any more able to run the communist movement than he was able to run his domestic life. In fact, nothing he tried in life worked very well. If Darwin's theory had not given scientific respect to a materialistic (no God) philosophy, Marx's communism would have been as studiously ignored in the twentieth century as it was during his lifetime.

Without doubt, though, the most important and widespread misconception about communism had to do with its image as a force for justice and equality. Marx apparently did not know how to think in those terms; or, if he did know how, he never let such thoughts guide his philosophy.

In 1848, the year of the "Manifesto," Marx was advocating

> ... the disarming of the bourgeoisie ... revolutionary terror ... and the creation of a revolutionary army.... Liberty is dismissed as a purely bourgeois ideal....[69]

Indeed, as Laski makes abundantly clear, Marx envisioned no picnic when the communists took over. The revolutionary government would

> ... have neither time nor opportunity for compassion or remorse. Its business is to terrorize its opponents into acquiescence. It must disarm antagonism by execution, imprisonment, forced labor, control of the press....[70]

Is this the far-seeing, all-wise prophet of the new and better world that communists say must inevitably come? What, basically, is different in this scheme from any totalitarian view of the past where a minority group forces its will on the majority? Marx, very much like Hitler, for example,

> ... was openly contemptuous of democracy ... throughout Marx's writings there is the assumption that reliance must be placed upon a class-conscious minority. For in his view there is no place in history for the majority principle.... Communists must proceed upon the assumption that nothing matters save the enforcement of their will.[71]

As to where all of this was supposed to lead; as to the nature of the reward for submitting to such a tyranny, Marx had little to say. He spoke vaguely of the state withering away, but he never gave any estimate as to how long that would take. In fact,

> ... he was always emphatic that the future must settle itself.[72]

In short, as Sidney Hook and others have demonstrated, Marx did not care how his system worked, or if it worked. He was no utilitarian. He promised no happiness.[73]

Now, a century and a quarter after "The Communist Manifesto," one may rightly marvel at the fact that Marx is still widely revered as some sort of champion of justice and fair play, some sort of kindly old scientist toiling selflessly for a perfect society. The only explanation for Marx's continued vogue among those who basically realize that his views were tyrannical, is that such utter absurdity makes sense in a world made utterly absurd by evolutionary thought. Anyone who cares to look can see that Marxist communism offers merely to trade one set of exploiters (the capitalist elite of his day) for another set (the communist elite of our day). His new exploiters promise violence, terror, oppression of body and mind, and certain and final extinction at death. Even the old exploiters were better than that. In any case, the old exploiters were simply an unforeseen but not unnatural result of the industrial revolution (which was not brought about by class struggle, incidentally). The worst of their offenses were well on their way toward being solved through unionization and government reforms before Marx had been in his grave very long. Today in the United States and several other countries all the real evils of capitalist exploitation were overcome decades ago, a development the Marxian "science" said was impossible.

The long and short of it all, in fact, is that Marxian

communism has been proven by actual history to be an absurd philosophy. Though flushed by its recent Southeast Asian victories, and though undoubtedly on an accelerated march today (so much so that Secretary of State, Henry Kissinger recently was reported to have said in private: "All Europe will go Marxist within 10 years."),[74] communism is, nevertheless, very sick inside. Authors are being harassed, imprisoned, and tortured once again for criticizing the system.[75] The government is finding it necessary to resort to increased controls and restrictions to keep captive the minds and bodies of those over whom it rules. A new escape-proof barrier 840 miles long has been built to keep East Germans from going to the West.

> East German authorities are reinforcing the deadly barrier. In recent months, for example, workmen have been methodically replacing the barbed wire fences with new gratings; their mesh is too fine to climb.
>
> Such grim improvements in the barrier are clearly designed to discourage East Germans, 871 of whom escaped last year, from interpreting *detente* as a license to flee to the West.... The East Germans have now equipped sections of the barrier with automatic self-firing weapons, mounted on three levels so that anyone seeking to jump the fence will trigger a shower of bullets.
>
> Where there are no self-firing weapons, second and third fences have been laid behind the frontier barrier with buried mines and a deep concrete-plated ditch between them. This type of fortification is intended to prevent a favorite escape maneuver: crashing through the barricade with a heavy car. Along certain sections of the border,

> the fences farthest away from the frontier are now equipped with electrified barbed wire that, when touched, alerts nearby border-control posts by optical and acoustical signals. Floodlights along populated sections of the frontier have long afforded West Germans a permanent panorama of escape attempts. Although such attempts have become suicidal, they are expected to continue. From now on, however, the new double barricades will help hide the spectacle from Western eyes.[76]

The essence of Marxism-Leninism is its *atheism*. All Communist Party members must be atheists. Though these party members make up only 3 or 4 percent of the total population, they control everything. Their anti-God philosophy is the core of their system. Their mission is to get rid of the idea of God in the world. This is what motivates and galvanizes them above all else. This is what gives them their missionarylike zeal to uproot past traditions, to throw out completely God and religion. At bottom, communism is a fanatic secular religion out to destroy the concept of God in the minds of men.

But—and this is the main point—evolution theory is absolutely necessary to modern communism's scientific-materialism; its atheism. Without evolution theory to explain that man and the universe got here by accident, atheistic communism could not have gotten to where it is in the world today. Moreover, without evolution theory to provide a seemingly logical rationale for its ideology of scientific-materialism, communism cannot continue as a credible alternative in the world today.

In short, evolution theory is the Achilles heel of communism. Destroy the theory (which has no scientific or logical standing whatever, as you have seen) and communism will cease to have any semblance of rationality for anyone able to think at all.

One can't be a communist without being an atheist, and one can't be an atheist, after all, if there is a logically proven God. And that is exactly the situation when evolution theory is removed as an explanation of man's origin (as you can verify in the "Philosophy" section).

Evolution theory *is* the Achilles heel of communism.

Philosophy

Philosophy is a word that does not lend itself readily to factual analysis. Yet there are certain things that are true about all philosophies and all philosophers. We shall list a few of these common denominators in order to better see where man's thoughts have taken him so far, and where those thoughts should likely go in the future.

I. All major philosophers from Socrates to Sartre have talked about God. In their thoughts on the subject they have basically taken one of three possible positions:

- God does not exist.
- God exists, but does not take any interest in His creations.
- God exists, and does take a direct interest in His creations.

It is an unusual fact, we think, that even the few philosophers who deny God's existence are compelled to speak and write so much about what they say doesn't exist. There almost seems to be a part of the mind that is set aside for thinking about God. It is a part that can be repressed or diverted, but not locked out completely. Primitive people offer evidence that something of the sort is true—not only for philosophers and all other "civilized" people—but for them as well. Harlow Shapley, for example, notes:

> I've learned from anthropologists that every primitive tribe, without exception, has a religion. . . . So religious belief is built into us as part of a reaction against mysteries we can't solve easily.[77]

II. Philosophers have had a far greater impact on the running of the world and on the lives of most people than would seem possible from their small numbers and their usual lack of economic and political power. This has been true because they have influenced the thinking of educated people who *did* have economic and political power. The average person in past centuries could not read, and the average literate person today does not read or study philosophy. Just the same, people who influence other peoples' lives economically, religiously, politically, militarily, legally, artistically, sexually, educationally, and in other ways, have definite philosophies which they transmit and instill by whatever means they can. The thinking of philosophers thus affects peoples' lives whether or not those people are aware of a particular philosophy or philosopher.

III. However exalted and brilliant a philosopher's thoughts may be, they are still the opinions of one person. The books that person has read, people he has known, experiences he has had, the quality of his love life, and a multitude of other things make up that opinion. His thoughts reflect his tastes, his fears, his digestion, his religion or lack of it, his teachers, parents, relatives, and his disposition; indeed, his total culture.

Some philosophers' opinions are shaped more by religious thought than by anything else. Some are shaped more by the importance and glory of the state, the strength of the military, and so forth. Wealth and position gained by competition in the market place shape others' philosophies. Concern for the welfare of workers, or the underprivileged, may be the main factor shaping a philosophy. Humanitarian concerns (through scientific means increasingly since 1500) may be the strongest determinant of a philosopher's opinion. Any of these five value orientations (religious, patriotic, money, common man, or humanist) or some combination of the five may shape a philosopher's opinions. But they are still opinions.

IV. Everyone, each in his own way, is a philosopher. Everybody has opinions about life and death, and quite a few of the experiences that come between being born and dying. Each person's opinions may not be as systematic or as explicit as those of a trained philosopher. But he can find a philosopher who is in general agreement with *anything* about which he might have an opinion.

V. One of the thousands of things that makes man so unique is his ability to hold abstract thoughts (opinions, philosophies) in his mind and to govern his behavior by those thoughts. Moreover, man can pass on his experiences, as no animal can. Huxley acknowledges this fact:

> Man is able to transmit the results of his experience, his knowledge, his ideas, cumulatively from generation to generation, which no animal can do.[78]

But more important and more unique is man's capability for rejecting one kind of philosophy and adopting another. It is not common to do so but man can change philosophies significantly if there is sufficient motivation to do so. That motivation could be truth, or money, or fear, or love, or other important things. Whatever the cause, man has the mentality to weigh realities, and consciously decide to change. He may make these changes on the basis of subjective experience, an act that defies evolutionists' explanations. As Huxley admits:

> ... the real nub of evolution, the aspect which is still the most mysterious, is the fact of subjective experience....[79]

People who have philosophies (built from their total life experience) that are negative often have good reasons why they have the outlook they do. It may also be understandable if their approach to life is to get what they can while the getting is good, and so forth. This "after me, the deluge" philosophy; this "live for the moment" opinion of life; this "nothing really matters" thought, are all part of a negative view (which is a practical, but selfish, view) that has become commonplace with the spread of evolutionary theory. A "survival of the fittest" road sign posted on every turn in the highway of life can definitely color one's philosophy. When alternated with signs reading: "Life—Dead End," a positive philosophy becomes very difficult to maintain even though virtually everyone wants to be positive and happy. Many philosophers have had essentially negative philosophies, and that negativism has affected peoples' lives by the means already indicated.

So much, then, for the common denominators of philosophies and philosophers and how such thought has influenced us so far. The philosophic question before us now is: *What kind of new philosophy will the collapse of evolutionary theory demand?* A section in a philosophy book entitled "Why Prove That God Exists?" gives us a good place to start. The author begins:

> If the existence of God could be proved, finding a proof would surely be a major accomplishment. It

would answer a question that millions of ordinary human beings and scores of great thinkers have asked....[80]

It is now possible to prove that a Creator exists.

He cannot be *defined* but His existence can be logically proven.

This is how.

Let the letter *A* stand for the concept of evolution. God is represented by *B*. Other explanations for life and the universe equal *C*.

Look at it this way: There are only three possible headings under which the origin of life can be discussed.

They are:
    A = Evolution
    B = God
    C = All explanations other than A or B

Letter *A* is eliminated by the scientific evidence in Part II and by the logical evidence in Part III; evidence that will be compounded a thousandfold in the coming decade.

Thus we have:
    A = Evolution—this choice is now OUT
    C = All explanations other than A or B

We must now demonstrate that explanations or objections that claim to be letter *C* are not what they claim to be. We must demonstrate that there are no other explanations for life and the universe; that there is, in fact, no letter *C*.

These explanations or objections can be called categories. There are eight categories. In other words, there are eight kinds of arguments which someone may attempt to call *C*.

1. The first category includes this kind of explanation

or objection: "Who says anything *is* here?! Nothing exists. Everything is unreal. It is all a dream."

Response to the first category: This objection declares that there is no cause behind life and the universe because they don't exist. Nothing exists, it is said. Presumably "nothing" would include these particular objectors and their particular objections. Clearly these people and their objections have no meaning and, by their own terms, do not exist. In any case, when the theory of evolution is exploded, and a Creator logically proven, it is predictable that these people will want to exist again. And, wanting to, they will. Their position, after all, is just an inversion of the evolutionist's position. The evolutionist says, "Everything exists and it all came out of nothing." These objectors say, "Nothing exists and it all came out of everything (or nothing, as they are the same)." These positions are equally meaningless in any discussion which seeks an answer to the question, "From whence did life come?" Something that is meaningless arising out of "nothing" can hardly be admitted as an alternative explanation for anything, much less for everything, which is what is required of *C*.

2. A second category of objections can be summed up in comments of this nature: "Everything always was and always will be."

Response to the second category: Does anyone know of anything that always was or always will be? Do *you* know of anything that had no beginning? That will have no end? If you do think of something that makes sense to you—that isn't just some kind of partial answer like "time" or "space"—you can bet your life that the "something," the only thing, you can conceive of as being infinite, that is without beginning or end, will be God. And this is not letter *C;* it is *B*.

3. A third category is related to the second, but is not precisely the same. Its central thought is: "Man is immortal."

Response to the third category: You know you had a beginning. Your parents or anyone else in the world will confirm this. You know you are going to die. So you know you are not immortal physically. What, then, do you mean by immortal? If you can't be physically immortal, how *can* you be immortal? What's left? You would rather not say *soul?* You like *energy* better? What is energy? Is it some little electrical charge you have in you that leaves for unknown parts when you die? How would you *know* you were immortal if you just wound up in the battery of someone's electric toothbrush? Man doesn't even know what electrical energy is. It will be pretty difficult to find someone who believes that electrical energy is *aware* of life—the way a living person is. *If* the energy *is* aware, it could not be so without a Guiding Force. That would be God (and one might just as well call the energy in question a soul). If it is not aware, there is no immortality as that word is commonly understood.

As for immortality through reincarnation, the same argument applies as is in the "energy" concept. That is to say: If a given reincarnation—be it animal, vegetable, or mineral—is imagined to have human awareness, then it could not be so without a Guiding Force, that is, God. In other words, if beer truck driver, Clarence Klopdike, recently deceased, is now fully aware but has gotten into the form of some animal, plant, or mineral somewhere, then all would agree that an extraordinary, supernatural force (who might as well be called God) would have to be involved in getting Clarence's awareness to its new home. If everyone is going to come back as something else (and be aware that they are back!), then there must be a God to carry out the transfer. The immediate point then would seem to be that in order to believe in reincarnation or the transmigration of souls, one would have to believe in a supernatural power who can be given any name, but is herein referred to as God. Being driven thus by logic, the believer in reincarnation has one more task, namely, that he must then decide if a God so powerful and unlimited would choose reincarnation as His way of giving mankind immortality....

Whatever the merits of this thinking (along with Nirvana and other aspects), it is clear that it is not letter *C* for which we are searching. Nor is it *A* (evolution). It is *B*.

4. A fourth category centers around the thought that: "Man *is* God." Or, "I am God."

Response to the fourth category: Create something! Not a paper clip or a piano. Create a tree or water or salt. You can't do it? Of course you can't. But it has been done.... You may not be God, but you have enough of God in you to know the difference between you and *B*. And no one, it would seem, could be so vain as to forget *that* difference once he realizes it.

5. A fifth category says: "God cannot be proven. He is beyond man's ability to prove."

Response to fifth category: He is beyond man's ability to define, but He can be logically proven. If there is an *A* and a *B*, and you can eliminate *A*, and you can't find a *C* that makes any sense, you are left with *B*, and all further argument is rendered useless (which is the definition of logic). The fact that some one thing (B) is shown to remain by argument is one of the definitions of *proof*. Hence, there is logical proof of God's existence.

6. A sixth category says: "God may be known, but only by subjective experience."

Response to sixth category: This category is difficult to work with. It requires close scrutiny. First, there are two certainties inherent in the statement: 1) There is no controversy over God's existence. God (letter *B*) is confirmed by the statement itself which states that there is a God, and that He can be known. 2) To make this statement, one of three things must be true: a) one must have had a subjective experience and thus be a person who knows God; or b) one must imagine or feel that this is the only way to know God, but does not actually know that the statement is true; or c) one may *feel* there is a God and want to *know* so strongly as to have subjectively experienced Him.

Another aspect of this category centers on the word "known."

"Known" to exist? Or "known" in the sense of being well-acquainted? The first meaning (known to exist) will be possible for all with the collapse of evolutionary explanations. The second meaning (known in the sense of being well-acquainted) is subjective. Each individual can define his acquaintance with God, but he cannot prove that acquaintance; he cannot prove subjective experience.

Thus, as can be seen, this category can lead readily down interesting paths; paths too labyrinthine and too speculative for this essay, however. The only issue is whether any of these categories suggest another explanation for life. Evolution (*A*) does not; others (*C*) cannot be found. This category, to stick to the main purpose, leaves one as it started, in other words, with God (*B*).

7. A seventh category of objection to God as the explanation for life on earth (after evolution is reduced to

a myth), is this: "Maybe we (or life) came from another planet in another galaxy."

Response to the seventh category: If life couldn't evolve here, then it couldn't have evolved anywhere else. No objection to this statement will hold up. This category is letter *A*, evolution; or letter *B*, God. It is not letter *C*. There is no letter *C*.

8. An eighth category of objection can be seen in the assertion: "Letter *C* will be found! Just because it hasn't been discovered yet, doesn't mean it won't be. So don't tell *me* I have to accept *B* (God) if evolution (*A*) is destroyed!"

Response to eighth category: This objection suggests that something which cannot even be *imagined* by all the people who ever lived will one day come forward as a non-God explanation for life, the earth, and the rest of the universe. It is possible for one to imagine extremely exotic causes for life on earth. One could imagine, for example, that the earth and all that is on it is merely a dissertation project worked out by a Ph.D. candidate at some super university in some other galaxy. This may put a bit of strain on one's imagination, but it can be imagined. Yet, it answers nothing, satisfies nothing. One is simply forced to imagine where the Ph.D. candidate came from, and so on back to the first cause argument (which is no argument really, since what could be The First Cause except God? Logically or illogically?).

Still, one can certainly demand the right to believe in some other unimaginable explanation (*C*) if one insists on that right. The only thing is that this person should realize as he waits on the super-unimaginable (*C*) to be discovered that he already has an explanation that accounts for everything, he just finds it too unimaginable!

Do you understand?! God is too unimaginable for him; yet he looks for something, *anything* that will be either more unimaginable or less unimaginable. Think of that.... More unimaginable (harder to imagine) than God? What could that be? The Ph.D. at Intergalactic University? Little green people from another time dimension? But these are not more unimaginable than God because if one wishes to attribute the universe and all that is in it to such a cause, it would *be* God (and few will want to be so flippant about defining God when they reach this stage!).

What, then, of something less unimaginable (easier to imagine) than God? What could that be? Evolution, of course! It is so much easier to imagine than God! Yet, remember two things: One, there was an indescribably intricate and balanced universe, including earth, *before* life began, none of which is explained or even imagined by evolutionary theory. Too, even this poor effort by amateurs has demonstrated that evolution is more unimaginable (harder to imagine) than God. Evolution has lost its usefulness as something easier to imagine than God. That was the role it was fulfilling as it turns out, but now that it (evolution) has been proven scientifically and logically impossible, one can only believe in it as a conscious expression of an unwillingness to believe in God under any circumstances. When the full meaning of all this sinks in, it is predictable that few will choose to be so vain and so defiant.

Letter *B* (God) becomes, then, not only the logical alternative to evolution as an explanation for life, it also becomes the only *il*logical alternative.

Those who reject logic as a tool for proving God's existence, insist that there is something beyond logic. Perhaps. But, if so, it can only be *il*logic that lies beyond logic. Since (after evolution is exploded) God is the only concept that is at once the most logical and the most illogical explanation for all that is, it is futile to look further in either direction.

In the opening paragraph of this chapter it was pointed out that there are three basic positions that philosophers have taken on the question of God. The first of these was: God does not exist.

That position is now eliminated.

The second position: God exists but does not take any interest in His creation.

This position with its eighteenth-century Deism, clockwinder theories, and the like, once served as transition philosophies between unquestioned, ritualized faith and modern day agnosticism and atheism. With God's existence logically (and illogically) confirmed, this position may well enjoy a transitory revival; but this time, the tide will be moving the other way, back toward unquestioning faith in God with strong but doubtless altered roles for organized religions.

Philosophy—somewhat discredited along with the natural and social sciences for its uncritical ride on the evolution bandwagon—no doubt will have a much more positive message as it moves from nihilism toward the logic of God, a logic which will be irresistible to mankind.

Final Comment

Evolutionary theory has been shown to be impossible. It is not even a theory. It is not a workable hypothesis. It must be discarded by rational people as an explanation for the origin of life.

Creation theory has been shown to be the only *possible* explanation for the origin of life. As there are two kinds of impossibilities—those that can be proven impossible, such as evolution, and those that merely seem impossible, such as creation—it can also be said that creation theory has been shown to be the *only "impossible"* explanation for the origin of life. Accordingly, rational people must contemplate life and the universe on the premise that there is a Creator.

It is difficult to comprehend the sweeping changes that will result from the single act of destroying evolutionary theory. Fortunately, all or virtually all of these changes will be of the most pleasant and positive nature. Because this is so, the potential that now exists for increasing mankind's happiness is a joy to contemplate. Barring destructive acts by some people who cannot bear to think that life is not absurd, profound new understandings can be expected in all areas of life. Moreover (though some will not wish it) profound new understandings of the mysteries of creation and the Creator are certain to come.

Indeed, by an extraordinary and totally unexpected set of circumstances, the demise of the theory of evolution promises to set man on the path to realizing his purpose at last. The Truth—a proven God—will be his beacon.

NOTES

Part Two

1. Louis Levine, *Review Notes in Biology* (New York: Monarch Press, Inc., 1963), p. 106.

2. Sol Tax and Charles Callender, eds., *Issues in Evolution* (Chicago: The University of Chicago Press, 1960), p. 76.

3. Ibid., p. 75.

4. Ernest Borek, *The Code of Life* (New York and London: Columbia University Press, 1965), p. 69.

5. Ibid.

6. Ibid.

7. Ibid., pp. 69-70.

8. Jay E. Greene, ed., *100 Great Scientists* (New York: Simon & Schuster, Inc., 1964), p. 126.

9. Walter E. Lammerts, "Discoveries Since 1859 Which Invalidate the Evolution Theory," *Creation Research Society 1964 Annual* (2717 Cranbrook Rd., Ann Arbor, MI, 1964), p. 1.

10. Julian Huxley, *Evolution in Action* (New York: Harper & Bros., 1953), p. 38.

11. Ibid., p. 35.

12. Ibid., p. 47.

13. Ibid., p. 39.

14. John J. Fried, *The Mystery of Heredity* (New York: The John Day Co., 1971), pp. 135-36.

15. Julian S. Huxley, et al. (including Dobzhansky, Niebuhr, Reiser, Nikhilananda), *A Book That Shook the World: Anniversary Essays on Charles Darwin's Origin of Species* (Pittsburgh: University of Pittsburgh Press, 1958), p. 17.

16. Maurice Caullery, *Genetics and Heredity* (New York: Walker and Co., 1964), p. 10.

17. Ibid.

18. Ibid., p. 119.

19. Ibid.

20. Ernst Mayr, *Animal Species & Evolution* (Cambridge, MA: The Belknap Press of Harvard University Press, 1963), p. 7.

21. Ibid., p. 176.

22. George Gaylord Simpson, *The Major Features of Evolution* (New York: Columbia University Press, 1953), p. 96.

23. Mayr, *Animal Species*, p. 179.

24. Ibid., p. 8.

25. Huxley, et. al., *Book That Shook the World*, p. 21.

26. George W. Burns, *The Science of Genetics—An Introduction to Heredity* (New York: The Macmillan Co., 1969), p. 291.

27. Ibid., p. 119.

28. Mayr, *Animal Species*, p. 236.

29. George Gaylord Simpson, *Life of the Past* (New Haven: Yale University Press, 1953), p. 142.

30. Henry L. Plaine, ed., *Darwin, Marx, and Wagner: A Symposium* (Columbus: Ohio State University Press, 1962), pp. 38-39.

31. Loren Eiseley, *The Immense Journey* (New York: Random House, 1957), pp. 83-84.

32. Ibid., p. 84.

33. Joseph Wood Krutch, "Lost Certainties," *Reporter*, (28 May 1959), p. 41.

34. Huxley, *Evolution in Action*, pp. 36-37.

35. Mayr, *Animal Species*, p. 7.

36. George Gaylord Simpson, *The Geography of Evolution* (Philadelphia and New York: G. P. Putnam's Sons, 1965), jacket of book.

37. Ibid., p. 17.

38. Sir Gavin De Beer, *Charles Darwin* (Garden City, NY: Doubleday & Co., Inc., 1964), p. 192.

39. Watchtower Bible & Tract Society of Pennsylvania, *Did Man Get Here by Evolution or by Creation?* (Brooklyn: Watchtower Bible and Tract Society of New York, Inc. and International Bible Students Assn., 1967), p. 68.

40. Ibid., p. 67.

41. Simpson, *Major Features*, pp. 118-19.

42. Huxley, *Evolution in Action*, p. 48.

43. Ibid., pp. 54-55.

44. Ibid., p. 46.

45. Simpson, *Geography of Evolution*, p. 14.

46. Milton S. Lesser, *Review Text in Life Science* (New York: Amsco School Publications, Inc., 1967), p. 201.

47. Simpson, *Major Features*, p. 340.

48. Amram Scheinfeld, *Your Heredity and Environment* (Philadelphia and New York: J. B. Lippincott Co., 1965), p. 585.

49. De Beer, *Charles Darwin*, p. 1.

50. Simpson, *Major Features*, p. 381.

51. Simpson, *Life of the Past*, pp. 143, 149-50.

52. Fried, *Mystery of Heredity*, pp. 59-60.

53. Borek, *Code of Life*, p. 194.

54. Rutherford Platt, "DNA the Mysterious Basis of Life," *The Reader's Digest*, (October 1962), p. 148.

55. Ibid., p. 144.

56. Fried, *Mystery of Heredity*, p. 131.

57. Borek, *Code of Life*, p. 216.

58. Fried, *Mystery of Heredity*, p. 131.

59. E. B. Ford, *Ecological Genetics* (London: Chapman & Hall Ltd., 1971), p. 106.

60. Simpson, *Major Features*, pp. 120, 121, 289, 355.

61. Norman Macbeth, *Darwin Retried: An Appeal to Reason* (Boston: Gambit Inc., 1971), p. 52.

62. Fried, *Mystery of Heredity*, pp. 9-10.

63. Ibid., p. 10.

64. John L. Tumey and Meidon E. Levine, "Genetic Engineering," *Saturday Review* (5 August 1972), p. 24.

65. "Invit: The View from the Glass Oviduct," *Saturday Review* (30 September 1972), p. 68.

66. Ibid.

67. William J. Tinkle, *God's Method in Creation* (Nutley, NJ: Craig Press, 1973), p. 29.

68. Robert C. King, *Genetics* (New York: Oxford University Press, 1965), p. 353.

69. John N. Moore, *Should Evolution Be Taught?* (San Diego: Institute for Creation Research, 1971), p. 5.

70. Charles Darwin, *The Origin of Species* (New York: P. F. Collier & Son Co., 1909), pp. 359-61.

71. Walter Sullivan, "Evolution: A New Concept," *New York Times* (25 October 1964), p. 8 E.

72. W. Brian Harland and Martin J. S. Rudwick, "The Great Infra-Cambrian Ice Age," *Scientific American* (August 1964), pp. 34, 35, 36.

73. Moore, "Should Evolution Be Taught?" p. 6.

74. Norman Macbeth, "The Question: Darwinism Revisited," *Yale Review* (June 1967), p. 618.

75. Garrett Hardin, *Nature and Man's Fate* (New York: Rinehart Co., Inc., 1959), p. 260.

76. Macbeth, "The Question: Darwinism Revisited," p. 629.

77. Ibid.

78. Henry M. Morris; William W. Boardman, Jr.; and Robert F. Koontz, *Science and Creation: A Handbook for Teachers* (San Diego: Creation Science Research Center, 1971), p. 14.

79. Watchtower, *Did Man Get Here by Evolution?* pp. 93-94.

80. "Science Exposes Fakes," *Science News Letter* (25 February 1961), p. 119.

81. Robert Silverberg, *Scientists and Scoundrels: A Book of Hoaxes* (New York: Thomas Y. Crowell Co., 1965), p. 232.

82. Anatole G. Mazour and John M. Peoples, *Men and Nations—A World History* (New York and Chicago: Harcourt, Brace & World, Inc., 1961), p. 12.

83. Fred J. Schering and Ben Schupack, *Mastering Earth Science* (New York and Los Angeles: Oxford Book Co., 1963), pp. 208-09.

84. Ibid., pp. 177-78.

85. Watchtower, *Did Man Get Here by Evolution?* p. 93.

86. Marcellin Boule and Henri V. Vallois, *Fossil Men* (New York: The Dryden Press, 1957), p. 111.

87. Ibid., p. 3.

88. Ibid., p. 2.

89. "Upgrading Neanderthal Man," *Time* (17 May 1971), p. 76.

90. Ibid.

91. A. Hyatt Verrill, *The Strange Story of Our Earth* (New York: Fawcett Publications, Inc., 1956), p. 137.

92. "Upgrading Neanderthal Man," p. 76.

93. "The Emergence of Man," advertisement brochure by *Time-Life* Books, 1972, no page numbers used.

94. Ibid.

95. Ibid.

96. Harry L. Shapiro, "Louis S. B. Leakey, 1903-1972," *Saturday Review* (28 October 1972), p. 72.

97. William Bridgewater and Elizabeth J. Sherwood, eds., *The Columbia Encyclopedia* (New York: Columbia University Press, 1956), p. 1207.

98. Lincoln Garnett, "Where Evolution Stands Today," *Life* (19 October 1959), p. 103.

99. Macbeth, "The Question: Darwinism Revisited," p. 626.

100. Paul Ehrlich and Richard W. Holm, *The Process of Evolution* (New York and San Francisco: McGraw-Hill Book Co., Inc., 1963), p. 276.

101. Bridgewater and Sherwood, *Columbia Encyclopedia*, p. 1206.

102. Paul S. Henshaw, *This Side of Yesterday: Extinction or Utopia* (New York: John Wiley & Sons, Inc., 1971), p. 65.

103. Lammerts, "Discoveries Since 1859," p. 1.

104. *Action Manual* (San Diego: Creation Science Research Center, 1972), p. 20.

105. "Was World Too Fast for Dino?" *The Miami Herald* (14 September 1972), p. 18 L.

106. James C. Southall, *The Recent Origin of Man* (Philadelphia: J. B. Lippincott & Co., 1875), p. 56.

107. Mayr, Animal Species, p. 6.

108. George Gaylord Simpson, The Major Features of Evolution, p. 351.

109. Ibid., pp. 351-52.

110. Ibid., pp. 352-53.

111. Ibid., p. 358.

112. Nicholas Hotton, III, The Evidence of Evolution (New York: D. Van Nostrand Co., 1968), p. 138.

113. American Geological Institute, Dictionary of Geological Terms (New York: Doubleday & Co., 1962), p. 72.

114. "The Bristlecone Correction," Scientific American (July 1970), p. 52.

115. Ibid.

116. Ibid.

117. Andre Boudin and Sara Deutsch, "Geochronology: Recent Developments in the Lutetium 176/Hafnium 176 Dating Method," Science (5 June 1970), p. 1219.

118. W. Gentner, "Fission Track Ages and Age of Deposition of Deep-Sea Microtektites," Science (17 April 1970), p. 361.

119. Schering and Schupack, Mastering Earth Science, p. 187.

120. Richard M. Pearl, 1001 Questions Answered About Earth Sciences (New York: Dodd, Mead & Co., 1962), p. 1.

121. Henry Faul, Ages of Rocks, Planets, and Stars (New York and St. Louis: McGraw-Hill Book Co., 1966), p. 32.

122. W. E. Le Gros Clark, The Fossil Evidence for Human Evolution (Chicago: The University of Chicago Press, 1955), p. 55.

123. R. N. C. Bowen, The Exploration of Time (London: George Newnes Ltd., 1958), p. 47.

124. Morris, Boardman, Koonst, Science and Creation, pp. 70-86.

Part Three

1. Watchtower Bible & Tract Society of Pennsylvania, Did Man Get Here by Evolution or by Creation? (Brooklyn: Watchtower Bible and Tract Society of New York, Inc. and International Bible Students Assn., 1967), p. 26.

2. Loren Eiseley, *The Immense Journey* (New York: Random House, 1957), p. 199.

3. J. Robert Moskin, "In the Next 25 Years Man Will Master the Secret of Creation," *Look* (16 January 1962), p. 46.

4. Jay E. Greene, ed., *100 Great Scientists* (New York: Simon & Schuster, Inc., 1964), p. 466.

5. Eiseley, *Immense Journey*, p. 200.

6. "Who Made It?" *Minnesota Technolog* (October 1957), p. 11.

7. Ernst Mayr, *Animal Species & Evolution* (Cambridge, MA: The Belknap Press of Harvard University Press, 1963), p. 625.

8. Collier's Encyclopedia (New York: Crowell-Collier Publications, 1971), p. 1206.

9. Amram Scheinfeld, *Your Heredity and Environment* (Philadelphia and New York: J. B. Lippincott Co., 1965), p. 585.

10. Ibid.

11. Vernon Reynolds, *The Apes* (New York: E. P. Dutton & Co., Inc., 1967), pp. 92-93.

12. Ibid., p. 93.

13. Ibid.

14. Ibid.

15. Ibid., p. 97.

16. C. R. Carpenter, *Naturalistic Behavior of Nonhuman Primates* (University Park: The Pennsylvania State University Press, 1964), p. 96.

17. Ibid., p. 97.

18. Ibid.

19. Errol E. Harris, *The Foundations of Metaphysics in Science* (New York: Humanities Press, 1965), p. 88.

20. John Napier, *The Roots of Mankind* (Washington, DC: Smithsonian Institution Press, 1970), p. 188.

21. Scheinfeld, *Your Heredity and Environment*, p. 585.

22. Ibid.

23. Julian S. Huxley, et al., *A Book That Shook the World: Anniversary Essays on Charles Darwin's Origin of Species* (Pittsburgh: University of Pittsburgh Press, 1958), p. 16.

24. Charles Darwin, *The Origin of Species* (New York: P. F. Collier & Son Co., 1909), p. 190.

25. Thomas Hunt Morgan, *A Critique of the Theory of Evolution* (Princeton: Princeton University Press, 1916), p. 32.

26. Nicholas Hotton, III, *The Evidence of Evolution* (New York: D. Van Nostrand Co., 1968), p. 138.

27. Henry L. Plaine, ed., *Darwin, Marx, and Wagner: A Symposium* (Columbus: Ohio State University Press, 1962), pp. 34-35.

28. Napier, *Roots of Mankind*, p. 11.

29. Plaine, ed., *Darwin, Marx, and Wagner*, p. 31.

30. Sol Tax and Charles Callender, ed., *Issues in Evolution* (Chicago: The University of Chicago Press, 1960), p. 43.

31. Ibid.

32. Mayr, *Animal Species,* back cover.

33. Ritchie Calder, *Science in Our Lives* (New York: The New American Library, 1954), p. 83.

34. Fred Hoyle, *The Nature of the Universe* (New York and Evanston: Harper & Row, Publishers, 1960), pp. 104-05.

35. Ibid., p. 105.

36. Ibid., pp. 67-68.

37. Frederick William Conner, *Cosmic Optimism: A Study of the Interpretation of Evolution by American Poets from Emerson to Robinson* (Gainesville: University of Florida Press, 1949), p. 41.

38. Maurice Caullery, *Genetics and Heredity* (New York: Walker and Co., 1964), p. 42.

39. Ibid., p. 43.

40. Ibid., p. 119.

41. Eldon J. Gardner, *Principles of Genetics* (New York and London: John Wiley & Sons, Inc., 1968), p. 146.

42. Norman Macbeth, "The Question: Darwinism Revisited," *Yale Review* (June 1967), pp. 622-23.

43. Gertrude Himmelfarb, *Darwin and the Darwinian Revolution* (New York: Doubleday & Co., Inc., 1962), p. 386.

44. Ibid., p. 390.

Part Four

1. Paul Ehrlich and Richard W. Holm, *The Process of Evolution* (New York and San Francisco: McGraw-Hill Book Co., Inc., 1963), p. vii.

2. Theodosius Dobzhansky, *Mankind Evolving—The Evolution of the Human Species* (New Haven and London: Yale University Press, 1962), p. xi.

3. Hunter A. Dupree, "The Book That Made Man Timeless: *Origin of Species,*" *Saturday Review* (14 November 1959), p. 61.

4. Dr. Etheridge, "Evolution Still Unproven," *The Miami Herald* (17 November 1972).

5. Ernest Borek, *The Code of Life* (New York and London: Columbia University Press, 1965), p. ix.

6. Jerry R. Tompkins, ed., *D-Days at Dayton* (Baton Rouge: Louisiana State University Press, 1965), jacket.

7. William J. Keeton, "Evolution: Basic to Biology," *Christian Century* (18 January 1967), p. 76.

8. Ibid.

9. Dupree, "Book That Made Man Timeless," p. 73.

10. Joseph Wood Krutch, "Lost Certainties," *Reporter,* (28 May 1959), p. 41.

11. D. S. Winnail, "Why the Growing Disenchantment with Science?" *The Plain Truth* (November 1972), p. 17.

12. Ibid.

13. Ibid., p. 20.

14. John Dewey, *Reconstruction in Philosophy* (New York: The New American Library, 1950), back cover.

15. Bert James Loewenberg, *Darwinism—Reaction or Reform?* (New York: Rinehart & Co., Inc., 1957), p. 52.

16. Ibid.

17. Ibid., p. 55.

18. Krutch, "Lost Certainties," p. 41.

19. Joseph Jastrow, *The House That Freud Built* (New York: Greenberg, 1932), p. 228.

20. Giovanni Castigan, *Sigmund Freud—A Short Biography* (New York: The Macmillan Co., 1965), jacket.

21. Paul Roazen, *Freud: Political and Social Thought* (New York: Alfred A. Knopf, Inc., 1968), p. 10.

22. Castigan, *Freud*, jacket.

23. Robert F. Davidson; Arthur L. Funk; Thomas A. E. Hart; and William Ruff, eds., *The Humanities in Contemporary Life* (New York: The Dryden Press, 1955), p. 342.

24. Castigan, *Freud*, jacket.

25. Fritz Wittels, *Freud and His Time* (New York: Liveright Publishing Corp., 1931), p. 4.

26. Ibid., pp. 4-5.

27. Ibid., p. 47.

28. Davidson, et al, eds., *Humanities in Contemporary Life*, p. 345.

29. Jastrow, *House That Freud Built*, p. 290.

30. Rousas J. Rushdoony, *Freud* (Philadelphia: Presbyterian and Reformed Publishing Co., 1965), p. 25.

31. Ibid., pp. 26, 27.

32. Sigmund Freud, *The Future of an Illusion* (Garden City, NY: Doubleday & Co., Inc., 1953), p. 102.

33. Sigmund Freud, *The History of the Psychoanalytic Movement*, ed. by Philip Rieff (New York: Collier Books, 1963), p. 11.

34. Ibid.

35. Stanislav Andreski, "Science As Sorcery," *Time* (25 September 1972), p. 71.

36. Erich Fromm, *Beyond the Chains of Illusion—My Encounter with Marx and Freud* (New York: Simon and Schuster, 1962), p. 33.

37. Reuben Osborn, *Freud and Marx—A Dialectical Study* (New York: Equinox Co-operative Press, Inc., 1937), p. 113.

38. Lester Velie, "The War on the American Family," *The Reader's Digest* (January 1973), p. 109.

39. Osborn, *Freud and Marx*, p. 120.

40. Ibid., p. 238.

41. Ibid., p. 28.

42. Ibid.

43. Ibid., pp. 28-29.

44. Richard King, *The Party of Eros* (Chapel Hill: The University of North Carolina Press, 1972), p. 8.

45. Paul A. Robinson, *The Freudian Left* (New York, Evanston, and London: Harper & Row, Publishers, 1969), p. 229.

46. King, *The Party of Eros*, p. 150.

47. Robert Ardrey, "Ignoble Savages," *Saturday Review* (14 October 1972), pp. 73-75.

48. Ronald L. Meek, ed., *Marx and Engels on Malthus* (New York: International Publishers Co., Inc., 1954), p. 171.

49. Gertrude Himmelfarb, *Darwin and the Darwinian Revolution* (New York: Doubleday & Co., Inc., 1962), p. 398.

50. J. D. Bernal, *Marx and Science* (New York: International Publishers, 1952), p. 17.

51. Oswald Spengler, *The Decline of the West* (New York: Alfred A. Knopf, Inc., 1926), vol. 1, p. 370.

52. Otto Rühle, *Karl Marx—His Life and Work* (New York: The New Home Library, 1926), p. 366.

53. Jacques Barzun, *Darwin, Marx, Wagner—Critique of a Heritage* (Garden City, NY: Doubleday & Co., Inc., 1958), p. 196.

54. Meek, ed., *Marx and Engels on Malthus*, p. 60 (cf. Laski, fn. 59).

55. Barzun, *Darwin, Marx, Wagner*, p. 192.

56. Wilhelm Liebknecht, *Karl Marx—Biographical Memoirs* (Chicago: Charles H. Kerr & Co., 1908), p. 26.

57. Edward Hughes, "Why the Soviet Union Can't Feed Itself," *The Reader's Digest* (April 1973), p. 150.

58. Rühle, *Karl Marx*, pp. 383-84.

59. Harold J. Laski, *Karl Marx: An Essay* (London: The Fabian Society, 1925), p. 27.

60. Rühle, *Karl Marx*, p. 150.

61. Ibid., p. 157.

62. Laski, *Karl Marx*, p. 27.

63. Rühle, *Karl Marx*, pp. 280-91.

64. Ibid., pp. 382-83.

65. Barzun, *Darwin, Marx, Wagner*, pp. 189-90.

66. Laski, *Karl Marx*, p. 17.

67. Barzun, *Darwin, Marx, Wagner*, p. 177.

68. Rühle, *Karl Marx*, pp. 306-07.

69. Laski, *Karl Marx*, p. 19.

70. Ibid., p. 39.

71. Ibid.

72. Ibid., p. 40.

73. Sidney Hook, *Towards the Understanding of Karl Marx* (New York: The John Day Co., 1933), p. 98.

74. "Washington Whispers," *U.S. News & World Report* (5 May 1975), p. 8.

75. "Crackdown on Dissent," *Time* (18 December 1972), pp. 31-34.

76. "East German Border Barriers," *Time* (22 January 1973), p. 33.

77. Sol Tax and Charles Callender, eds., *Issues in Evolution* (Chicago: The University of Chicago Press, 1960), p. 48.

78. Ibid., p. 25.

79. Ibid., p. 48.

80. George Naknikian, *An Introduction to Philosophy* (New York: Alfred A. Knopf, Inc., 1967), p. 167.

APPENDIX

Edward Blyth

Edward Blyth "outlines very clearly the theory of natural selection in all its details. We may be quite sure that the journal in which these essays appeared in 1835, '36, and '37 was one that Darwin read dutifully from cover to cover, not only while he was on the voyage but afterward. It seems unthinkable that he could have missed these articles altogether; in fact, there is very good evidence that he did not. In 1842, '44, and '47, Darwin wrote notes and sketches of his theory in preliminary form. In those notes and preliminary abstracts, one finds him using certain odd words such as 'inosculate,' used not in the sense of kissing but of simple adjoining, and used by Darwin in the same particular context as Blyth had used the same odd word. We know, too, that in later years Darwin corresponded with Blyth, who went to India, that he thought very highly of Blyth as a thinker, and that he was particularly interested in his studies of animal variation. Yet never, in note or word or letter, and certainly not in publication, did Darwin make reference to the three essays by Edward Blyth on natural selection. The internal evidence seems completely convincing that he had read these and, maybe with a photographic memory, had registered what was in them. Why did he then make no reference to them? It may well have been because Blyth used the theory of natural selection not to explain how species arise from preexisting species, but rather to explain how species remain constant. The action of selection, he thought, would serve to eliminate not only monsters, but all deviants from the norm, all those abnormal types that arise in every population; and so it would make each species hold true to type, stay fit to continue its existence within the given environment. Darwin evidently absorbed Blyth's idea and turned it over in his own mind for a period of years, perhaps until he had completely forgotten where the idea originated. Then, by a brilliant stroke, he turned the theory upside down to say: 'Not only will natural selection keep species constant, it will also, if the environment varies, make the species vary to fit new environments' " (taken from *Darwin, Marx, and Wagner: A Symposium*, pp. 38-39).

Slime Hoax

The laying of the first trans-Atlantic cable in the 1860s "involves one of the most peculiar and fantastic errors ever committed in the name of science."

Evolutionary biologists, already in command a decade or so after Darwin's book came out, believed that the deep recesses of the oceans, "unchanging through the ages," would reveal "living fossils," actual missing links in the history of life. Thomas Huxley (Darwin's bulldog), then at the height of his powers, proclaimed with characteristic vigor:

> It may be confidently assumed that . . . the things brought up will . . . be zoological antiquities which in the tranquil and little changed depths of the ocean have escaped the causes of destruction at

work in the shallows and represent the predominant population of a past age.

Scientists—evolutionists and nonevolutionists alike—anticipated thrilling new finds as the *Challenger* steamed out of port in 1872 under the auspices of the British Admiralty and the scientific directorship of Sir Charles Thompson. "Sixty-nine thousand miles and four years later her weary scientists came home. They had rocked sickeningly in all seas, had dragged ... the very bowels of Creation. They had handled rare forms of life, looked at things denied to ordinary men.... Nevertheless, their eyes were empty...."

Why such cruel disappointment from plans so well laid and so enthusiastically championed by Huxley, Haeckel, Thompson, and others? The main reason is that the long expedition hadn't found "the great globe-girdling carpet of living ooze" that was thought to be the evolutionary base from which all life sprang.

"Haeckel in Germany and Huxley in England" had labored "to show that as one passed below the stage of nucleated single-celled organisms one arrived at a simple stirring of the abyssal slime wherein something that was neither life nor non-life oozed and fed without cellular individuality.

"This soft, gelatinous matter had been taken from the ocean bed during dredging operations. Examined and pronounced upon by Professor Huxley, it was given the name of *Bathybius haeckelii* in honor of his great German colleague. Speaking before the Royal Geographical Society in 1870, Huxley confidently maintained that *Bathybius* formed a living scum or film on the sea bed extending over thousands of square miles. Moreover, he expanded, it probably formed a continuous sheet of living matter girdling the whole surface of the earth."

The evolutionists were very excited. It looked as if they were about to unveil the very secret of life, a slime that consisted apparently "of an amorphous sheet of protein compound . . . capable of assimilating food . . . a diffused formless protoplasm . . . arising from non-living matter . . . their vital phenomena being traceable to physico-chemical causes." Here was the link of the living with the nonliving. Here in this "seething, unindividualized ooze whose potentialities included the butterfly and the rose . . ." man was also to find his beginning.

And, of course, they found not only no badly needed transitional link, they found no slime. It didn't exist! A member of the expedition on the *Challenger*, one Mr. Buchanan, found "as he tried to investigate the nature of the *Bathybius*, that he could produce all the characters of that indescribable animal by the simple process of adding strong alcohol to sea water." A specimen examined under a lens showed "that sulphate of lime was precipitated in the form of a gelatinous ooze which clung around particles as though ingesting them, thus lending a superficial protoplasmic appearance to the solution."

Mr. Huxley's original specimen had "apparently been treated in this matter when it was sent to him," and this energetic and eager evolutionist along with others of like mind "participated in what was, and remains, one of the most curious cases of self-delusion ever indulged in by scholars. It was the product of an overconfident materialism, a vainglorious assumption that the secrets of life were about to be revealed." (The facts and much of the wording were taken from Loren Eiseley's book, *The Immense Journey*, pp. 34-40.)

The Bristlecone Correction

A long-lived California tree apparently holds the answer to a puzzle that has troubled students of ancient history for some years. This is the discrepancy between dates derived from historical evidence and dates derived from carbon-14 measurements: the historical dates are considerably older. The best-known instance is found in Egypt. There the dynastic lists of kings made it possible to date the First Dynasty with confidence around 3000 B.C. Carbon-14 analysis of First Dynasty materials, however, suggests that they are five hundred years younger.

The tree is the bristlecone pine, a slow-growing evergreen found on the barren slopes of the White Mountains in central California. A series of overlapping tree-ring counts from various bristlecone specimens extends back in time for more than seven thousand years. The wood in each ring thus provides a sample of organic material with a known date that can be subjected to carbon-14 analysis. This has been done by Hans E. Suess of the University of California at San Diego. When the two series of dates are compared, the carbon-14 underestimation of age increases with the increase in the true age of the specimen.

Reviewing other recent efforts to correlate historical and carbon-14 chronologies, the editors of *Current Archaeology* report that carbon-14 analysis of organic material from Egyptian tombs of various known dates shows discrepancies that agree generally with Suess's findings. They also note that students of medieval archaeology have found a carbon-14 "wobble" that affects dates in the sixteenth and seventeenth centuries: carbon-14 analysis of wood from tree rings that were formed in A.D. 1520 and 1640 both yield the same date: 1570.

Suess's bristlecone studies show similar wobbles; there are several between 1800 and 2500 B.C. and earlier ones around 3000 and 3600 B.C. The causes of the underestimation and the wobbles are not yet understood (*Scientific American,* July 1970, vol. 223, no. 1, no author).

Miscellaneous Evolutionary Humor

Comedians can probably do more to finish off the evolution theory than any other single group. The material is ready made and available by the carload at libraries all over the country—or the world, for that matter. People have almost forgotten how to laugh because of the humorless and clammy and ceaseless indoctrination by evolutionists. They are waiting stolidly serious in their cocoons, ready to be turned into butterflies by the comedian's deft play upon evolutional absurdities. The potential for a great cathartic universal joke is immense, for never, *never,* has there been an intellectual flimflam so complete in its success, so deadly to the human spirit, and yet so imminently illogical and downright laughable as the theory of evolution.

We call upon comedians to roll up their sleeves, spit on their hands and go to work on the dour, unsmiling world of human animals that evolutionists have bequeathed us. Heresy and blasphemy, humorously delivered against the evolutionists religion which no one likes but most accept, would be knee-slappingly funny to millions.

Pretentious sounding theoretical concepts could be blown up to their greatest possible inflation, and then punctured with sharp verbal pins that would make all mankind laugh. Evolutionary religion is so droll, so vapid, so joy limiting. The notion that humans like other placental mammals " . . . all started as small shrewlike creatures and have adaptively radiated into such diverse types as bats, armadillos, rats, whales, cats, cows, men, and a thousand others" has got to do something sick to your view of life. Unless, that is, comedians present the evolutionary "facts"! Then all of us can have some fun out of the stuffy intellectual mongoloid after all.

Material for comedians is abundant, as we mentioned. We recommend turning to the index of any book designed to advance the theory of evolution, and picking out items that seem suited to one's particular style. From "adaptive radiation" through "saltation," from "chromosomes" and "eugenics" through "Neanderthal Man" and "Drosophila melanogaster" there is a rich vein of humor to be mined, and there is a public "out there" in grave need of this natural resource.

BIBLIOGRAPHY

Action Manual. San Diego: Creation Science Research Center, 1972.

American Geological Institute. *Dictionary of Geological Terms.* New York: Doubleday & Company, Inc., 1962.

Andreski, Stanislav. "Science As Sorcery." *Time,* 25 Sept. 1972.

Ardrey, Robert. "Ignoble Savages." *Saturday Review,* 14 Oct. 1972.

Barzun, Jacques. *Darwin, Marx, Wagner—Critique of a Heritage.* Garden City, N.Y.: Doubleday & Company, Inc., 1958.

Bernal, J. D. *Marx and Science.* New York: International Publishers, 1952.

Borek, Ernest. *The Code of Life.* New York and London: Columbia University Press, 1965.

Boudin, Andre and Deutsch, Sara. "Geochronology: Recent Development in the Lutetium 176/Hafnium 176 Dating Method," *Science,* 5 June 1970.

Boule, Marcellin and Vallois, Henry V. *Fossil Men.* New York: The Dryden Press, 1957.

Bowen, R. N. C. *The Exploration of Time.* London: George Newnes Limited, 1958.

Bridgewater, William and Sherwood, Elizabeth J., eds. *The Columbia Encyclopedia.* New York: Columbia University Press, 1956.

Burns, George W. *The Science of Genetics: An Introduction to Heredity.* New York: The Macmillan Company, 1969.

Calder, Ritchie. *Science in Our Lives.* New York: The New American Library, 1954.

Carpenter, C. R. *Naturalistic Behavior of Nonhuman Primates.* University Park: The Pennsylvania State University Press, 1964.

Castigan, Giovanni. *Sigmund Freud—A Short Biography.* New York: The Macmillan Company, 1965.

Caullery, Maurice. *Genetics and Heredity*. New York: Walker and Company, 1964.

Clark, Robert T. and Bales, James D. *Why Scientists Accept Evolution*. Grand Rapids: Baker Book House, 1966.

Clark, W. E. Le Gros. *The Fossil Evidence for Human Evolution*. Chicago: The University of Chicago Press, 1955.

Collier's Encyclopedia. 1971.

Conner, Frederick William. *Cosmic Optimism: A Study of the Interpretation of Evolution by American Poets from Emerson to Robinson*. Gainesville: University of Florida Press, 1949.

"Crackdown on Dissent." *Time*, 18 December 1972.

Davidheiser, Bolton J. *Evolution and the Christian Faith*. Nutley, NJ: Presbyterian and Reformed Publishing Company, 1969.

_____. *To Be As God*. Nutley, NJ: Presbyterian and Reformed Publishing Company, 1972.

Davidson, Robert F.; Funk, Arthur L.; Hart, Thomas, A. E.; Ruff, William, eds. *The Humanities in Contemporary Life*. New York: The Dryden Press, 1955.

Darwin, Charles. *The Origin of Species*. New York: P. F. Collier & Son Company, Inc., 1909.

De Beer, Sir Gavin. *Charles Darwin*. Garden City, N.Y.: Doubleday & Company, Inc., 1964.

Dewey, John. *Reconstruction in Philosophy*. New York: The New American Library, 1950.

Dobzhansky, Theodosius. *Mankind Evolving—The Evolution of the Human Species*. New Haven and London: Yale University Press, 1962.

Droscher, Vitus B. *The Mysterious Senses of Animals*. New York: E. P. Dutton & Company, Inc., 1965.

Dupree, Hunter A. "The Book That Made Man Timeless: *Origin of Species*." *Saturday Review*, 14 November 1959.

"East German Border Barriers." *Time*, 22 January 1973.

Ehrlich, Paul R. and Holm, Richard W. *The Process of Evolution*. New York and San Francisco: McGraw-Hill Book Company, Inc., 1963.

Eiseley, Loren. *The Immense Journey*. New York: Random House, 1957.

Etheridge, Dr. "Evolution Still Unproven." *The Miami Herald*, 17 November 1972.

Faul, Henry. *Ages of Rocks, Planets, and Stars*. New York and St. Louis: McGraw-Hill Book Company, 1966.

Fichtner, Margaria. "The Elephant in Her House." *The Miami Herald*, 24 August 1972.

Ford, E. B. *Ecological Genetics*. London: Chapman & Hall Ltd., 1971.

Freud, Sigmund. *The Future of an Illusion*. Garden City, N.Y.: Doubleday & Company, Inc., 1953.

Fried, John J. *The Mystery of Heredity*. New York: The John Day Company, 1971.

Fromm, Erich. *Beyond the Chains of Illusion—My Encounter with Marx and Freud*. New York: Simon and Schuster, 1962.

Gardner, Eldon J. *Principles of Genetics*. New York and London: John Wiley & Sons, Inc., 1968.

Garnett, Lincoln. "Where Evolution Stands Today." *Life*, 9 October 1959.

Gentner, W. "Fission Track Ages and Ages of Deposition of Deep-Sea Microtektites." *Science*, 17 April 1970.

Gish, Duane T. *Evolution?—The Fossils Say No!* San Diego: Creation-Life Publishers, 1972.

Greene, Jay E., ed. *100 Great Scientists*. New York: Simon & Schuster, Inc., 1964.

Hardin, Garrett. *Nature and Man's Fate*. New York: Rinehart & Company, Inc., 1959.

Harland, W. Brian and Rudwick, Martin J. S. "The Great Infra-Cambrian Ice Age." *Scientific American*. August 1964.

Harris, Errol E. *The Foundations of Metaphysics in Science*. New York: Humanities Press, 1965.

Henshaw, Paul S. *This Side of Yesterday: Extinction or Utopia*. New York: John Wiley & Sons, Inc., 1971.

Himmelfarb, Gertrude. *Darwin & the Darwinian Revolution*. New York: Doubleday & Company, Inc., 1962.

Hook, Sidney. *Towards the Understanding of Karl Marx*. New York: The John Day Company, 1933.

Hotton, Nicholas III. *The Evidence of Evolution*. New York: Doubleday & Company, Inc., 1962.

Hoyle, Fred. *The Nature of the Universe*. New York and Evanston: Harper & Row, Publishers, 1960.

Hughes, Edward. "Why the Soviet Union Can't Feed Itself." *The Reader's Digest*. April 1973.

Hughes, Phillip E. *The Control of Human Life*. Nutley, NJ: Presbyterian and Reformed Publishing Company, nd.

Huxley, Julian. *Evolution in Action*. New York: Harper & Brothers, 1953.

____, et al. *A Book That Shook the World: Anniversary Essays on Charles Darwin's Origin of Species*. Pittsburgh: University of Pittsburgh Press, 1958.

Jastrow, Joseph. *The House That Freud Built*. New York: Greenberg, 1932.

"Invit: The View from the Glass Oviduct." *Saturday Review*, 30 September 1972.

Keeton, William J. "Evolution: Basic to Biology." *Christian Century*, 18 January 1967.

King, Richard. *The Party of Eros*. Chapel Hill: The University of North Carolina Press, 1972.

King, Robert C. *Genetics*. New York: Oxford University Press, 1965.

Krutch, Joseph Wood. "Lost Certainties." *Reporter*, 28 May 1959.

Lammerts, Walter E. "Discoveries Since 1859 Which Invalidate the Evolution Theory." *Creation Research Society 1964 Annual*. San Diego: Creation Science Research Center, 1964.

____, ed. *Scientific Studies in Special Creation*. Nutley, NJ: Presbyterian and Reformed Publishing Company, 1971.

____, ed. *Why Not Creation?* Nutley, NJ: Presbyterian and Reformed Publishing Company, 1970.

Laski, Harold J. *Karl Marx: An Essay*. London: The Fabian Society, 1925.

Lee, Francis N. *Communism Versus Creation*. Nutley, NJ: Presbyterian and Reformed Publishing Company, 1969.

Lesser, Milton S. *Review Text in Life Science*. New York: Amsco School Publications, Inc., 1967.

Levine, Louis. *Review Notes in Biology*. New York: Monarch Press, 1963.

Liebknecht, Wilhelm. *Karl Marx—Biographical Memoirs*. Chicago: Charles H. Kerr & Company, 1908.

Loewenberg, Bert James. *Darwinism—Reaction or Reform?* New York: Rinehart & Company, Inc., 1957.

Macbeth, Norman. *Darwin Retried: An Appeal to Reason*. Boston: Gambit Incorporated, 1971.

____. "The Question: Darwinism Revisited." *Yale Review*, June 1967.

Mayr, Ernst. *Animal Species & Evolution.* Cambridge, MA: The Belknap Press of Harvard University Press, 1963.

Mazour, Anatole G. and Peoples, John M. *Men and Nations—A World History.* New York and Chicago: Harcourt, Brace & World, Inc., 1961.

Meek, Ronald L., ed. *Marx and Engels on Malthus.* New York: International Publishers Company, Inc., 1954.

Moore, John N. *Should Evolution Be Taught?* San Diego: Institute for Creation Research, 1971.

____ and Slusher, Harold S. *Biology: A Search for Order in Complexity.* Grand Rapids: Zondervan Publishing House, 1970.

Morgan, Thomas Hunt. *A Critique of the Theory of Evolution.* Princeton: Princeton University Press, 1916.

Morris, Henry M. *Biblical Cosmology and Modern Science.* Nutley, NJ: Presbyterian and Reformed Publishing Company, 1969.

____. *Evolution and the Modern Christian.* Nutley, NJ: Presbyterian and Reformed Publishing Company, 1967.

____. *The Twilight of Evolution.* Grand Rapids: Baker Book House, 1963.

____; Boardman, William W., Jr.; Koontz, Robert F., *Science and Creation: A Handbook for Teachers.* San Diego: Creation Science Research Center, 1971.

Moskin, J. Robert. "In the Next 25 Years, Man Will Master the Secret of Creation." *Look,* 16 January 1962.

Naknikian, George. *An Introduction to Philosophy.* New York: Alfred A. Knopf, Inc., 1967.

Napier, John. *The Roots of Mankind.* Washington, D.C.: Smithsonian Institute Press, 1970.

Osborn, Reuben. *Freud and Marx—A Dialectical Study.* New York: Equinox Cooperative Press, Inc., 1937.

Pearl, Richard M. *1001 Questions Answered About Earth Science.* New York: Dodd, Mead & Company, 1962.

Plaine, Henry L., ed. *Darwin, Marx, and Wagner: A Symposium.* Columbus: Ohio State University Press, 1962.

Platt, Rutherford. "DNA the Mysterious Basis of Life." *The Reader's Digest.* October 1962.

Reynolds, Vernon. *The Apes.* New York: E. P. Dutton & Company, Inc., 1967.

Rieff, Philip, ed. *Sigmund Freud: The History of the Psychoanalytic Movement.* New York: Collier Books, 1963.

Roazen, Paul. *Freud: Political and Social Thought.* New York: Alfred A. Knopf, Inc., 1968.

Robinson, Paul A. *The Freudian Left.* New York, Evanston, and London: Harper & Row, Publishers, 1972.

Rühle, Otto. *Karl Marx—His Life and Work.* New York: The New Home Library, 1929.

Rushdoony, Rousas J. *Freud.* Philadelphia: Presbyterian and Reformed Publishing Company, 1965.

Scheinfeld, Amram. *Your Heredity and Environment.* Philadelphia and New York: J. B. Lippincott Company, 1965.

Schering, Fred J. and Shupack, Ben. *Mastering Earth Science.* New York and Los Angeles: Oxford Book Company, 1965.

"Science Exposes Fakes," *Science News Letter,* 25 February 1961.

Shapiro, Harry L. "Louis S. B. Leakey, 1903-1972." *Saturday Review,* 28 October 1972.

Shute, Evan. *Flaws in the Theory of Evolution.* Nutley, NJ: Presbyterian and Reformed Publishing Company, 1961.

Silverberg, Robert. *Scientists and Scoundrels: A Book of Hoaxes.* New York: Thomas Y. Crowell, 1965.

Simpson, George Gaylord. *Life of the Past.* New Haven: Yale University Press, 1953.

_____. *The Geography of Evolution.* Philadelphia and New York: Chilton Books, 1965.

_____. *The Major Features of Evolution.* New York: Columbia University Press, 1953.

Southall, James C. *The Recent Origin of Man.* Philadelphia: J. B. Lippincott & Company, 1875.

Spengler, Oswald. *The Decline of the West.* Vol. I. New York: Alfred A. Knopf, Inc., 1926.

Standen, Anthony. *More Sacred Cows—Little Heresies in America and Elsewhere.* New York: William Morrow and Company, 1962.

Sullivan, Walter. "Evolution: A New Concept." *New York Times,* 25 October 1964.

Tax, Sol and Callender, Charles, ed. *Issues in Evolution.* Chicago: The University of Chicago Press, 1960.

"The Bristlecone Correction." *Scientific American.* July 1970.

"The Emergence of Man." Advertisement brochure by *Time-Life Books,* 1972.

Tompkins, Jerry R. *D-Days at Dayton.* Baton Rouge: Louisiana State University Press, 1965.

Tumey, John L. and Levine, Meidon E. "Genetic Engineering." *Saturday Review*, 5 August 1972.

"Upgrading Neanderthal Man." *Time*, 17 May 1971.

Velie, Lester. "The War on the American Family." *The Reader's Digest*, January 1973.

Verrill, A. Hyatt. *The Strange Story of Our Earth*. New York: Fawcett Publications, Inc., 1956.

"Was World Too Fast for Dino?" *The Miami Herald*, 14 September 1972.

Watch Tower Bible & Tract Society of Pennsylvania. *Did Man Get Here by Evolution or by Creation?* Brooklyn: Watchtower Bible and Tract Society of New York, Inc. and International Bible Students Association, 1967.

Whitcomb, John C., Jr. *The Early Earth*. Grand Rapids: Baker Book House Company, 1972.

____. *The World That Perished*. Baker Book House, 1973.

____ and Morris, Henry M. *The Genesis Flood*. Presbyterian and Reformed Publishing Company, 1961.

"Who Made It?" *Minnesota Technolog*, October 1957.

Winnail, D. S. "Why the Growing Disenchantment with Science?" *The Plain Truth*, November 1972.

Wittels, Fritz. *Freud and His Time*. New York: Liveright Publishing Corporation, 1931.